Aaron Ja... ...Cole's

GET LOST!

the cool guide to

Amsterdam

Get Lost Publishing, 2012

British Library in Publication Data. A catalogue record for this book is available from the British Library.

Get Lost Publishing, February 2012

ISBN: 978-90-76499-00-0

For all their help, advice, information, inspiration and support, many thanks to...

Aaron, Adam, Anthony and Nina, Arnie &Tia, Betts family four, Bulum family, Brent, Dave
David, Derma Donna, DNA, Don, Doug, Dugan fams, E-fans, Egg, Ellen, Franck, Gen
Green Compassion Collective (Riverside CA), Grey Area (& all the fossils) The Headshop
Hempworks, Jamie, Jaro, Jon, John, Joseph, Julian, Kim, Kokopelli, Kristin, Larry, Laura
and Alan, Lies, Lin, Mark, Martijn, Mike's Bikes crew (all of you!), Misty & Fams, Mollie
Mom and Pop Cole, Mama and Papa van Drimmelen, Paige, Patrick, Phoenix, Pink Point
Red, Richard, Roland & Tinne, Rosana, Stef, Steve, Super Dude,Texas Mike, Tijmes &
Zeraya, Tim, Trey,Tumbleweed Cartel, Vanessa, Village Grind in Wrightwood CA, Wavy
Davy ...Extra special thanks and love to my darlings Saskia and Jadie Moon: and Joe and
Lisa who made this book possible.

Edited by... **John Sinclair**

Cover design and layout .... **Ellen Pauker**

Photos ....**Patrick Weichselbaumer**
Aaron James Cole
Joe Pauker
Saskia van Drimmelen
(Thanks to **Zeraja Terluin** for the bathtub tower photos'

Printed with vegetable-based inks
on post consumer recycled paper.

Introduction

Congratulations! You have wisely decided to visit the world's coolest city.
Despite a wild reputation, Amsterdam is a relaxed place, a little big city vibrant with culture, a welcome oasis of sanity in our increasingly mad world. And, yes, it can be as wild as you desire—or as chilled out and sedate.

When I moved here the city wowed me with its dynamic underground music and art scenes. An autonomous international subculture was thriving in squatted 18th-century buildings, warehouses and abandoned grain silos where concerts, cheap cafés, art events and multi-media parties were held. Everything was accessible to everyone and I couldn't resist staying; Amsterdam became my adopted home.

I now have the privilege of continuing *Get Lost!* started by my good friends Joe and Lisa to share information about Amsterdam's coolest places with friends and fellow travellers. This new 12th edition has been completely revised and updated with lots of new hot spots and the latest Amsterdam happenings. It continues to be an independent DIY project. We've sold some ads to help pay for the printing and the paper but nobody pays to be included in *Get Lost!*

Amsterdam changes all the time. I've tried to correctly report prices, opening times, phone numbers and websites, but I can be a spacer, so send us a mail if you have any updates, suggestions, criticisms or donations. There will be regular updates on places and *Cool Guide* info, with links to various shops on our website: (www.getlostguide.com).

Thanks for buying *Get Lost!*
and have a great trip!

Aaron James Cole

Contents

Places to Sleep...7
Hostels 8
Hotels & Guest Houses.............................10
Camping 15

Getting Around................................**16**
Bicycles 16
Inline Skates 19
Electric Mopeds and Segways 19
Cars 20
Boats 21
Ferries...22

Map of Amsterdam **24-5**

Getting Out of Amsterdam **26**
Train 26
Bus 26
Hitching...26
Air Travel...27
Train to the Airport 28
Taxi to the Airport 28
Maps & Travel Books 28

Practical Shit...................................**29**
Tourist Info..29
Money 29
Phone 30
Post...30
Left Luggage..31
Voltage..31
Weather...31
Drinking Water.......................................31
Tipping...32
Toilets..32
Free English News...................................32
Recycling 32
Laundry..32
Identification Laws 33
Pickpockets..33
Drug Testing...33
Smoking Ban 34
Gay & Lesbian Info 34

Food..**35**
Supermarkets 35
Health Food Stores 36
Street Foods 38
Night Shops & Late-Night Eating..............41
Bread 42
Free Samples..43
Breakfast 43
Restaurants 45

Cafés **56**

Cannabis **62**
Coffeeshops 63
Seeds & Grow Shops 68
Hemp Stores 69
Headshops 70
Cannabis Competitions 70

Shopping **72**
Markets 72
Books & Magazines 74
Records & CDs 78
Used Clothing Stores 80
Tattoos and piercing 80
Haircuts 82
Chocolate 82
Smart Shops & 'Shroom Vendors 84
Miscellaneous 85
Free Postcards 87

Hanging Out **88**
Parks 88
Public Squares 89
Libraries 90
Internet Cafés 91
Free Concerts 91
Snowboarding & Skateboarding 92
Disc Golf & Kite Flying & Juggling 93
Tower Climbing & View Gazing & Cloud Gazing 94
Saunas & Massage Therapy 95
Swimming Pools 95
Beaches 96
Street Festivals 96
Kids 97

Museums & Galleries **101**
The Unusual Ones 101
The Big Ones 105
Out of Town 107

Music **108**
How To Find Out Who's Playing 108
Live Music & Party Venues 109
Dance Clubs 115
Music Festivals 116
Musicians & Street Performance 118
Underground Radio 119

Bars **120**

Film **128**
Cinemas 128
Miscellaneous Film Stuff 132

Sex **134**
Sex Shops 134
Peep & Live Sex Shows, Miscellaneous Sex Stuff 136

Dictionary **139**

Phone Numbers **142**
Emergency & Health 144
General Info Lines, Embassies & Consulates 146

Index **148**

About the Author

Aaron James Cole spent his youth knee-deep in snow, leading to a life long love of winter. Once, while crossing a perilous, high sierra pass, he lost his way. Frosbit and starving, he contemplated self-cannibalism until a Sasquatch family rescued and befriended the young explorer. After a few months, fully recovered, he made a vow to protect the Bigfoot family's secret location and descended down the mountain. He later perpetrated hairy-suited hoaxes to mislead the public, including the famous "Bigfoot Stretching" video, the moves boosted from a Jane Fonda workout tape. After hitch-hiking several times back and forth across America, he landed in Michigan where he became the "Kalamazoo Karaoke Champion" winning local folks' hearts with a stirring rendition of Olivia Newton John's "Let's Get Physical." Nicknamed "Kid Kalamazoo" by fans, this enigmatic crooner currently haunts Karaoke bars worldwide—you might catch him at one near you.

Places to Sleep

Accommodation is one of the most expensive parts of a trip to Amsterdam. Rooms have always been relatively expensive and rate increases are frequent. There's an abundance of luxury hotel rooms, but budget-minded travellers don't have as many options. It can really suck trying to find a room, particularly in the busy summer months, or for short visits. Here are some tips:

During the summer, a bed in a hostel runs anywhere from about €18 to €35, and a clean double room for less than €90 is a good deal. In the winter (except around holidays) prices can drop considerably, especially on weekdays.

Bed & Breakfasts are springing up around town, some with just a couple of rooms. Due to Amsterdam's accommodation shortage the city is offering incentives to people starting B & Bs, which are usually much more affordable than hotels. Sleep At Amy's, located in an 18th-century house on Haarlemmerdijk 26, is a friendly place run by an American couple. Rooms go for around €35 per person per night. You can find them and other B & Bs at *www.absoluteamsterdam.com*.

The Amsterdam Tourist Office (a.k.a. the VVV), across the square in front of Centraal Station and to your left, or in the station on Platform 2 has a room-finding service. They can book you a dorm bed or a hotel room, but the cheap ones go fast, of course. You pay the full amount at the tourist office plus a €3.50 per person service charge. The people who work at the Tourist Office are very nice and sometimes you can get a good deal, but in high season the line-ups are painfully long and slow. Open: Mon-Sat 8-20; Sun 9-17.

The Amsterdam Hotel Service (Damrak 7, 520-7000; *www.amsterdamhotelservice.com*), just across the street from Centraal Station, offers last-minute specials on all categories of hotels. They charge a €3 per person booking fee. You prepay 10% of the room cost there, and the other 90% at the hotel. Open: Daily 9-21.

The GWK bank (627-2731) in Centraal Station also offers a room-finding service. There you pay a whopping €9.75 per room fee and the full amount of the hotel in advance. The fact that you can't see the place first is a drawback, but their "same-day" sell-off rates (on all grades of hotels) are sometimes a real bargain, especially off-season. Open: Daily 8-22.

There are dozens of online hotel booking agents. CityMundo (*www.citymundo.nl*) books **apartments and houseboats** all over the city. The rates are comparable to those of a quality hotel, but then you've got your own place with all the comforts of home.

Finally, wherever you stay, and no matter how safe the place seems, never leave your valuables lying around. Keep your important stuff with you or, even better, leave it in a safety-deposit box if your hotel has one.

hostels

Schiphol Airport

www.schiphol.nl

Schiphol is one of the best airports in the world in which to sleep. If you have an early flight, crashing here is a good way to save the cost of a night's lodging. They have comfortable couches in the departure lounges where you can actually lie down and sleep (that's in the boarding area, not in the rest of the airport). This area is accessible to passengers only until midnight: if you don't get there before, it's plastic chairs or on the floor. Before you check in, hit the Food Village supermarket (open daily 6-24) on the arrivals level for the cheapest edibles. Feel like a pint of Guinness before snoozing? Near gate D10 is Murphy's Irish Pub, open until 21:00 in low season and 22:00 in high season. For all you soap dodgers there are free showers next to the British Airways lounge (like the good couches, they're in the boarding area). Or for €12.50 you can have a more luxurious bathing experience in a private cabin with soap, towel, and a hair dryer at the Hotel Mercure (604 1339) near gate "F". For breakfast croissants and coffee are the norm for around €5. If you're broke there are often free cheese samples laid out at the duty-free delicatessen. And upstairs, in the Panorama Lounge, they sell a few reasonably priced snacks. Schiphol is constantly expanding and always has new eating spots, like an Italian-style coffee, sandwich and pasta joint called Per Tutti with pretty good quality eats. Prices are usually steep, like in most airports, so it's worth having a wander and checking out what deals are on offer. As for intellectual nourishment, visit the free Rijksmuseum exhibition where ten major paintings from their collection are on permanent display.

The Flying Pig - Nieuwendijk 100, ☎ 420-6822; Vossiusstraat 46, ☎ 400-4187

www.flyingpig.nl

The guys who run these places are travellers themselves, which explains things like the use of kitchens, late-night bars, free internet access, and the absence of curfews. For hanging out, both locations have lounges, and Nieuwendijk has DJs. All rooms have toilets and showers, and prices include a free basic breakfast. The hostel on Nieuwendijk (Flying Pig Downtown) is very close to Centraal Station. The rates per person for shared rooms with 4 to 22 beds range from €21 to €31.50. Couples can save money and have fun by booking an extra wide bunk bed which, depending on the size of the room, runs from €31 to €47 per bed. They also have a girls-only dorm. The other hostel (Flying Pig Uptown) is by Vondelpark. They have shared rooms with 4 to 10 beds for €20 to €29.50 per person, and double bunks from €29.50 to €45 per bed. A €10 cash deposit for sheets and keys is returned when you leave. Both sites are central, but the neighborhood around Vondelpark is nicer and, of course, next to the park. To reach the Uptown from Centraal Station take tram 1, 2, or 5 to Leidseplein. Walk across the bridge to the Marriott Hotel and turn left. The hostel is on the street that runs along the left side of the park. (Map areas D4, B8)

Coco Mama - Westeinde 18, ☎ 627-2454

www.cocomama.nl

This charming establishment is actually a "boutique hostel" but they do have private rooms. Coco Mama is the brainchild of two 20-something Dutch girls who offer a pleasing atmospheric alternative to the often grungy hostel world. Originally one of the city's oldest brothels, this monument to times past now contains a combination hostel/hotel with Dutch theme-inspired rooms. They've managed to preserve the building's splendor—old chandeliers hanging, original staircase with worn and chipped wood railing—while remaining clean and modern. The "Red Light Room" is decorated as an *hommage* to the building's former glory and features red-draped bunk beds plus nudie mag photo collages on the walls. The rooms sleep between 2 and 6 people and cost between €35-€51 per person in high season. All include in-room showers and toilets. In the downstairs lounge/kitchen guests have free coffee, tea and cereal plus pasta and rice. The 50s retro-style refrigerator is shared but includes a free shelf. Sometimes they serve food like on Tight Ass Tuesday—spaghetti and a beer for €2! Other bonuses include a remarkably friendly and helpful staff, a relaxed, roomy back garden, an old-school Nintendo console, bike rentals and boat excursions. This is not your average hostel. If Coco Mama's founders represent the future of hostelery, they're leading the way in style. This place is relatively small, so book in advance or you might not get a room! (Map area E8)

nternational Budget Hostel - Leidsegracht 76, ☎ 624-2784

www.internationalbudgethostel.com

Centrally located in an historic 17th-century Amsterdam warehouse, this hostel has a unique canal view—something usually reserved for more expensive lodging. The owner is also a traveller and offers a peaceful environment for weary backpackers. In high season rooms go for between €15 per person (shared 8-bed room) to €35 for a double. Breakfast is not included in the price but is available between 9-12 am. The common room has vending machines, a TV, a public phone, an internet station and is WiFi connected. No curfew here, but the reception closes at 23:00, so make advance arrangements if you're arriving in town late. (Map area C6)

Tourist Inn - Spuistraat 52, ☎ 421-5841

www.tourist-inn.nl

There's nothing fancy about this hostel, but it's a bit more spacious and clean than some of the others in the neighborhood around Centraal Station. Dorm beds cost from €20 in low season (that's okay) to €35 per person in high season (that's not). They have an elevator for those with screwed-up knees, and there's a TV and phone in every room. Breakfast is included. Doubles and triples are also available, but the price is too high for what they're offering. You can take trams 1, 2, 5, 13 or 17 and get off at the first stop. Or just walk from Centraal Station. (Map area D4)

Bob's Youth Palace - Nieuwezijds Voorburgwal 92, ☎ 623-0063

www.bobsyouthhostel.nl

You can usually find this hostel by looking for a bunch of backpackers sitting on the front steps, smoking joints and hanging out. This is a pretty cool place where a lot of travellers stay, but it's cheap, simple lodging: don't expect more than the basics. It's located in the city center and you get a dorm bed and breakfast for between €18 to €23. They also rent apartments complete with kitchens for €70 for two people. Bob's also has a women's dorm. Trams 1, 2, 5, 13 or 17 will take you there, or you can walk from Centraal Station: it's not far. (Map area D4)

International Youth Hostels - Zandpad 5 (Vondelpark), ☎ 589-8996
Kloveniersburgwal 97, ☎ 624-6832

www.stayokay.com

These are "official" youth hostels. The one in Vondelpark (a great location) has been completely renovated and all their rooms are equipped with toilet and shower. They offer dorm beds in larger rooms, depending on the season, from €20 to €27, and quad rooms from €25 to €30 per person. Double rooms cost €65 to €74 per room. Members receive a €2.50 discount. Sheets are included in the price, as is an all-you-can-eat breakfast. There are also restaurants, a bicycle rental service, internet facilities, and a tourist info center. And I've been assured that, most of the time, groups of kids on field trips will be booked into a different building from the one housing independent travellers. From Centraal Station take tram 1, 2, or 5 to Leidseplein. Walk to the Marriott Hotel and turn left. The hostel sign is just a block ahead of you. The other location is also nice: on a wide canal right in the center of the city, but there are only dorm rooms. Beds cost €20 to €24. (Map areas E6, B7)

places to sleep

Stay Okay - Timorplein 21, ☎ 551-3190

www.stayok.com

This hostel is located in East Amsterdam's *Indische buurt*, a bit far out of the center. The prices work on a sliding scale, depending on how full the place is. A bed in a spacious six-person room will run you between €20 and €22. If you want a two-person room it can be €28 to €46 per person, with breakfast included in the price. The rooms are clean and have a toilet and shower, a modern key-card system and 24-hour access. This place is massive (460 beds) but still books out in high season. A bar with half-price happy hour from 21:30-22:30 and Sunday night free big-screen Wii tournaments are some of the extracurricular amusements available. The place is completely wheelchair-accessible and has rooms designed for the disabled. Take tram 7 or 10, direction Javaplein. Right around the corner from Studio K (see Film). (Map area J7)

Hans Brinker Hotel - Kerkstraat 136-138, ☎ 622-0687

www.hans-brinker.com

The motto here: It Can't Get Any Worse. A reception desk carved with dozens of initials and a graffitied elevator that looks like a punk bar toilet add to the trashy appeal. You can book a bed during high season in a five-person room for around €28, including a locker. The rooms are relatively clean but not fancy. There's a restaurant with meals such as veggie lasagna for €6.50 and fish and chips for €6, which is cheap. €3 pints are available at the bar and there's an mp3 jukebox. Located near Leidsestraat. (Map area C6,7)

The Winston - Warmoesstraat 129, ☎ 623-1380

www.winston.nl

This funky hotel (see below) also has dorm beds for around €25 to €30. A continental breakfast is included. (Map area D4)

hotels and guest houses

Here are a few places with clean, reasonably priced rooms. In the summer you should try to arrange your accommodations in advance, or at least before leaving Centraal Station (see intro to this chapter for details). Expect prices to jump during holiday periods.

Hotel Rookies - Korte Leidsedwarsstraat 147, ☎ 428-3125

www.rookies.nl

All the rooms in this popular, centrally located hotel have private facilities, cable TV, a telephone, a safe, and reading lights. The building is 200 years old, but the interior is modern. Average prices per room: €85 for singles, €117 for doubles and €127 for a twin room with a bathtub – all include a full breakfast with scrambled eggs, cheeses, cold cuts, and fresh OJ. There's also a stylish townhouse available, complete with kitchen and small patio, that sleeps 6 and goes for about €40 per person. Run by the same people as The Rookies Coffeeshop (see Cannabis chapter), it's smoker-friendly, too. Take tram 1, 2, or 5 to Leidseplein and then it's just a short walk. (Map area C7)

Hemp Hotel Amsterdam - Frederiksplein 15, ☎ 625-4425

www.hemphotel.com

This little theme-based pension is totally unique--all five internationally inspired rooms are decked out in hemp. Try sleeping on a hemp mattress for a few nights in the Afghani room. Or, if you've always fancied a visit to the Himalayas, book the Indian room. Rates are €65 for a single, €70 for a double, €75 for a twin with private shower, and all include a vegetarian breakfast. An extra mattress in the room costs an additional €10. Look for a drop of about 10% off-season. Downstairs, you can party in the Hemple Temple bar until 3 on weeknights and 4 on Friday and Saturday. They serve hemp snacks, hemp beer, but alas, no more hemp vodka right out of the freezer. Take tram 4 from Centraal Station to Frederiksplein. (Map area E8)

Hotel Abba - Overtoom 122, ☎ 618-3058

www.abbabudgethotel.com

Hotel Abba is a friendly hotel located on the bustling Overtoom. Depending on the season, singles cost from €25 to €55. Doubles (some with a shower and toilet) range from €45 to €80. They also have rooms for 4 and 5 people that run from €25 to €35 per person, including an all-you-can-eat breakfast. The free safety deposit boxes in the reception area are a convenient feature: use them! There's a nice view from the front (especially from the upper floors). Smoker friendly. Close to Leidseplein and Vondelpark. Take tram 1 from Centraal Station to Constantijn Huygensstraat. (Map area A7)

Coco Mama - Westeinde 18, ☎ 627-2454

www.cocomama.nl

This charming establishment is actually a "boutique hostel" but they do have private rooms. (see Hostels for review).

Hotel Hortus - Plantage Parklaan 8, ☎ 625-9996

www.hotelhortus.com

Located near Amsterdam's historic botanical gardens is Hortus, a bargain hotel with lots of extra amenities. These include free WiFi and internet use, a vending machine stocked with beer, a free pool table, complimentary breakfast and even an in-house vaporizer for serious stoners. If you want to cook, Hortus also has kitchen facilities for guests. The common room is large and airy, with plenty of light. The prices are similar to a hostel (€25-€30 per person) and some of the rooms are laid out with multiple bunk beds, but you get to sleep in a quiet, central neighborhood. Employees here are notoriously friendly and will gladly answer your Amsterdam questions or show you how to use the vaporizer correctly. (Map area F6)

The Greenhouse Effect - Warmoesstraat 55, ☎ 624-4974

www.thegreenhouseeffect.com

The 17 rooms of this smoker-friendly hotel each have a different theme—outer space, tropical dream and Turkish delight—ideal for the stoner traveler who'll spend a bit more money on accommodation. Prices start at €75 for a single, €110 for a twin, €140 for triples and €180 for quads. Every room has a color TV and a safe, and most have a private shower and toilet. The price includes a breakfast buffet until noon, and guests are entitled to special happy-hour prices all day on weed and booze at the hotel's coffeeshop and bar downstairs. If you're traveling with a group, look into one of the three apartments they rent. The Greenhouse Effect is located in the Red Light District, which is walking distance from Centraal Station. (Map area D4)

Hotel Liberty - Singel 5, ☎ 620-7307

www.hotelliberty.nl

Hotel Liberty is in a petite old canal house in Amsterdam's historic center. Here you'll find very basic rooms with shared facilities for a great price. What makes this place unique is the hospitality. Molly, an enthusiastic Jack Russell terrier, will likely be the first to meet you, followed by the friendly folks who run the joint. The vibe here is like staying at someone's home— someone who's happy to share local knowledge on all things Amsterdam. The common area/office has coffee and tea, cooking facilities, a fridge plus some cool additional features— an X-box and a bong, ideal for stoner tournaments. Yep, they're smoker-friendly too. Here's another special feature: dogs are allowed, as long as their owners promise to clean up any accidental messes. Just a few minutes walk from Centraal Station. (Map area, D3,4)

St. Christopher's at The Winston - Warmoesstraat 129, ☎ 623-1380

www.winston.nl

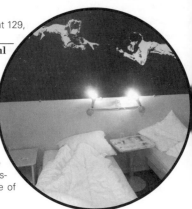

Over half of the Winston's rooms were designed by artists. Some are really fantastic, but others are super-ugly or sponsored by crappy corporations. Fortunately you can see pics of the rooms on-line before you make a booking. Depending on the season, prices range from €50 to €80 for singles, €65 to €100 for twins, €90 to €123 for triples, and €105 to €156 for quads. They also have dorm beds for €20 to €30. A continental breakfast is included, and there's a great club on the premises (see Music chapter) where hotel guests get half-off on admission. It's situated in the Red Light District just a couple of minutes from Dam Square. (Map area D4)

The Flying Pig - Nieuwendijk 100, ☎ 420-6822, Vossiusstraat 46, ☎ 400 4187

www.flyingpig.nl

Both these hostels have private rooms, too. Singles start at €60, and twins at €75. See the Hostels section (above) for more details.

Groenendael - Nieuwendijk 15, ☎ 624-4822

www.hotelgroenendael.com

If you prefer to stay close to the center of town, then this hotel is a good deal. Singles go for €35, doubles for €60, and triples for €90 (cheaper off season). Showers and toilets are in the hall. The rooms are tiny and pretty basic, but you're paying for the location. Breakfast is included, and there's a lounge where you can hang out and meet people. The shopping street where Groenendael's located on is a trifle sleazy, but not dangerous. From Centraal Station, walk or run. (Map area D3)

Hotel Aspen - Raadhuisstraat 31, ☎ 626-6714

www.hotelaspen.nl

There are a bunch of hotels in the beautiful art nouveau Utrecht Building. The hotel Aspen is a small, family-run place that feels more like a guesthouse than a hotel. Singles here start at €40. Doubles with a sink in the room start at €50. A triple with shower and toilet goes for €85 to €95. And a quad with shower and toilet is €100. No breakfast, but a great location close to Dam Square and the Anne Frank House. From Centraal Station take tram 13 or 17 to Westermarkt and walk back half a block. If you don't have much luggage, it's about a 15-minute walk. (Map area C4)

Bed & Coffee - Rustenburgerstraat 427, ☎ 065-519-4911

www.bedcoffee.nl

Because this tiny three-room guesthouse is a bit out of the center, you can stay here for a great price—the cost of a hostel dorm bed. But hostels don't feature "light art" in every room. Here you can choose from four special lighting options: black light, colored spots, psychedelic, or space. Obviously it's a smoker-friendly place. Prices vary from €40 - €100 per room. The shower and toilet are shared. It's very clean, and there's a cozy lounge with a TV, 24-hour internet access, and free coffee, tea, soup, and hot chocolate. Book very early. Bed and Coffee is located in the *Pijp* (Pipe) area. From Centraal Station take tram 24 or 25 to Ceintuurbaan, walk two blocks further along Ferdinand Bolstraat and turn right.

n Ostade Bicycle Hotel - Van Ostadestraat 123, 679-3452

www.bicyclehotel.com

If you're travelling by bicycle take note: this is one of the only hotels in Amsterdam with free indoor bike parking. They also rent bikes to guests and provide info on bicycle tours in and around Amsterdam. And they have recycling bins for glass and paper. That's cool. The rooms? €35-€70 for a single, €40- €120 for doubles, €60-€105 for triples and €80- €170 for a quad. Breakfast is included. The rooms aren't exciting, but they're clean and all have TVs. There's a library/lounge downstairs with free internet access. It's located in *De Pijp* – a fun, lively neighborhood crammed with bars, shops and restaurants. From Centraal Station take (or cycle behind) tram 24 or 25 and stop at Ceintuurbaan. Cross the street and go one block further.

otel Rembrandt - Plantage Middenlaan 17, ☎ 627-2714

www.hotelrembrandt.nl

Rembrandt is a sweet little hotel in a beautiful, wealthy area of town. All the rooms have private facilities, a TV and a coffee/tea maker, but if you've got the dough, splurge on the more expensive doubles (€115 per room). Each of those rooms is uniquely decorated, has a modern bathroom, and is way nicer than what you normally get for that price in Amsterdam. Other doubles cost €95 per night. Sometimes they can squeeze in an extra person for €25. Quad rooms cost €175. A free breakfast is served in an incredible antique-filled room. On weekends there's a minimum three-night stay. Book early! The Botanical Gardens (see Museums chapter) is two minutes away, and just beyond that is the Waterlooplein market. From Centraal Station take tram 9 to Plantage Kerklaan and then walk back half a block. (Map area F6)

oyd Hotel - Oostelijke Handelskade 34, ☎ 561-3636

www.lloydhotel.com

The Lloyd is a beautifully renovated monumental building located east of Centraal Station in the Eastern Docklands. It's billed as a "cultural embassy" and the rooms as well as the atmosphere are artistic. Accomodations range from one to five star quality, but each is unique. Prices go from €70 to a whopping €295. Some of the views are amazing. There's a café, bar, restaurant, library, ticket outlet, and a parking lot on the premises. It's close to the Bimhuis jazz center (see Music chapter) and the Cantine (see Bars). From Centraal Station take Tram 26 to Rietlandpark. (Map area I4)

mstel Botel - Oosterdokskade 24, ☎ 626-4247

www.amstelbotel.nl

This four-storey hotel-on-a-boat used to be in front of Centraal Station (CS) but has moved to Amsterdam North, near the NDSM terrain (see Music). It now takes a 10-minute ferry ride from behind CS to get to the Botel. It may seem a bit far, but this part of the North on the IJ waterway has a definite urban waterfront charm and a unique view of Amsterdam. The rooms here are small but very clean and modern. Each has a tiny shower and toilet, a phone, and a TV with free in-house videos (including a porn channel). The reception is open 24 hours and they don't charge commission to change your money. Single and double rooms cost €89 per room (€94 for a water view); triple rooms cost €119 (€124 for a water view). Breakfast is not included. Prices drop about €10 in the winter. A ferry goes to NDSM two times per hour (until midnight on weekdays and 1:00 on weekends), departing from directly behind CS. After that time, a free shuttle will bring you from the all-night ferry, which also departs behind CS, direction Buiksloterweg.

places to sleep

House-Boat Hotel

www.houseboathotel.

Like the idea of sleeping on an Amsterdam canal? Rent a houseboat. This website offers several boa
for daily or weekly rental. If you're travelling with a small group, houseboats can be comparable to t
price of a hotel but are usually more luxurious. These boats are very popular so make sure you bo
well in advance. There's a €20 booking fee. Note also that smoking is only allowed outside – on t
balconies or in the gardens.

Hotel Arena - 's Gravesandestraat 51, ☎ 694-7444

www.hotelarena.

Years ago, this huge old mansion was converted into a low-budget hostel because the City wanted h
pies to stop sleeping in Vondelpark. It turned into one of Amsterdam's coolest hostels, in spite of bei
located out of the Centrum. Iggy Pop even played their club in the mid 90s. Now the dorms are gone a
they only rent rooms. Depending on whether or not you want their expensive breakfast, doubles a
twins go for €80 to €175. Triples go for €135 to €202. All rooms have shower and toilet, TV, telephone, a
the very important reading lights by the bed. If you need a video game fix, you can rent a Playstation (€
for 24 hours) and there's WiFi access in some parts of the building. Breakfast is included, but not a 5
tax. As always, it's a good idea to make a reservation. It's close to the Tropenmuseum and Oosterpa
From Centraal Station take tram 9 to Mauritskade. Night bus 356. (Map area G8)

Xaviera Happy House - Stadionweg 17, ☎ 673-3934

www.xavierahollander.com/sleep

The Happy Hooker has a guesthouse: that had to be in The Cool Guide. I know that €120 a night is
exactly cheap, but this is the home of a real celebrity. Xaviera Hollander's house is in the wealthy ar
of Amsterdam south. She rents two rooms to visitors. Both have TVs and king size beds, and breakfa
is included. Prices sometimes drop in the off-season or for long stays. Go to the website to see p
tures of the rooms and to read about all the creative projects Xaviera's got going.

Black Tulip Hotel - Gelderskade 16, ☎ 427-0933

www.blacktulip.

I should start by saying that this hotel, situated in a 16th-century canal house near Centraal Statio
caters exclusively to leather men – that is, gay men who are seriously into S/M, B&D and leather fetis
Each of the nine luxurious rooms is decorated differently, but all feature kinky sex equipment: me
cages, stocks, fist-fuck chairs, etc. In addition to slings and bondage hooks, all rooms have TVs w
VCRs, minibars, telephones, and private bathrooms (some with whirlpool). Prices range from €1
to €195 and include a buffet breakfast in their comfortable lounge. And, as a service to guests w
prefer to travel light, they rent body bags, straight jackets, heavy leather boots and other paraphernal
(Map area E4)

Prins Hendrik Hotel - Prins Hendrikkade 53, ☎ 623-7969

www.hotelprinshendrik.

I've never been inside, but this is the hotel where Chet Baker died. He fell (or took a dive, or w
pushed) out of his window back in 1988. If you're a big fan you might want to stay here too, or -
you find that a tad morbid – check out the plaque in front commemorating one of jazz's late grea
(Map area E4)

camping

Camping Zeeburg - Zuider IJdijk 20, ☎ 694 4430

www.campingzeeburg.nl

They have all kinds of facilities here, including a funky bar that throws regular parties in the summer. Camping costs €11.50 per person during high season and €6.50 during low season. Camping site rates drop in price the more people you have in your group. There are also "camping huts" with beds at around €20 per person. Open all year. From Dam Square take Bus 22 (direction Indische Buurt) to the Kramatweg, or Tram 14 to the end of the line. From there you can follow the signs that lead you over the big bridge and to the campgrounds on the right. Night bus 359 (then a 20 minute walk).

Gaasper Camping - Loosdrechtdreef 7, ☎ 696 7326

www.gaaspercamping-amsterdam.nl

€5 per adult, €2.50 per kid, €2.50 per dog (plus €6 for a 2 person tent, €7 for a 3 or more person tent, and €4.50 per car). Open March 15th to November 1st. Take metro 53 from Centraal Station to Gaasperplas. From there it's a five-minute walk. Night bus 357.

Amsterdamse Bos - Kleine Noorddijk 1, ☎ 641 6868

www.campingamsterdamsebos.nl

There's a campsite here in the beautiful woods just south of the city center. €5 per person, €6 to €7 per tent, €4.50 per car. They also have basic, little cabins for about €10 per person, and more comfortable cottages that sleep five for about €25 per person. Open year round. Bus 172 from Centraal Station takes you to Amstelveen station where you transfer to bus 171 which takes you to the campground.

Vliegenbos - Meeuwenlaan 138, ☎ 636 8855

www.vliegenbos.com

This site is located in a wooded area of Amsterdam North. It costs €8 per person, and an extra €8 if you have a vehicle. There are also 30 cabins (four beds each) that rent for €70 a night. They accept written reservations for the cabins from March. Open from April 1st to September 30th. From Centraal station take buses 32 or 36. Night bus 361.

Getting around

Amsterdam's old city center, with its countless canals and cobblestone streets, is perfect place to wander and get lost. Getting found is easy—almost everyone speak English. The names of the streets, which often change every few blocks, can be daun ing to pronounce. Usually, if you point to a map a local can explain how to get whe you're going. A good city map costs about €2 and is a worthy purchase. The street names are a listed on the back, making it quick and easy to find the addresses in this book.

If you don't want to pay for a map, there are a variety of free maps available around town. Thes maps are often limited to the old Centrum but can be handy for finding coffeeshops (Cannab Retailers' Association and High View both make maps), tourist locations, and Gay tourist spots. Th Visitor Guide has a pretty good map. Gay tourist maps are free at Pink Point (see Practical Shi There's also a map in the front of the phone book, complete with a street index.

The city's basic layout, a series of horseshoe-shaped canals surrounding the oldest section, make it fairly easy to find your way on foot. Strolling Amsterdam streets, one can fully appreciate i unique beauty. Online, go to www.atlas.amsterdam.nl

Type in the street name and number of your hotel or any other place in Amsterdam you're lookin for and it loads a printable map of the street, neighborhood, or entire city with your destinatio clearly marked. Smartphone heads can always use GPS…but watch those roaming fees! So, no you know your way around town: **go get lost!**

Note: Sidewalks here can be miniscule; commonly giving visitors the misconception that walkir in the street is preferable. Dangerous decision. If you inadvertently step in front of local bicyclist they tend to ring their bells just before they hit you, allowing only a terrifying second to leap out the way or get nailed. And sympathy for your injured nervous system or bruised leg will be spars Try to stay on the sidewalk, no matter how absurdly small it may seem.

bicycles

Don't be scared to rent a bike and go for an authentic Amsterdam experience. Unlike most North American and many European cities, bikes are respected in Amsterdam. There are still an abundance of stinky, annoying cars, vans, scooters, trucks and taxis in the city center, but there are also thousands of fast, efficient bicycles. Bike lanes dominate the town and it's a fun, relatively safe way to explore.

Listed below are several places to rent bikes. If you're here for a while, consider buying a used bike and selling it when you leave. Make sure to lock your bike everywhere, even if you're only leaving it for an instant (see note on bike theft).

One of the cheapest places to buy a lock is the Waterlooplein flea market (see Markets, Shopping chapter).

Over the past couple of years, in an effort to "clean up the city" (whatever that means) there have been several crack-downs on illegal bike parking (I'm not joking). So if you see a sign that says *geen fietsen plaatsen* or *fietsen worden verwijderd*, or you notice that an area is conspicuously free of any other parked bikes, lock up somewhere else.

Parking is particularly difficult and enforcement is especially ruthless around Centraal Station. Make sure you use the free multi-level bike parking lot at the west side of the station, or if you don't mind paying €1.10 for the service, park at one of the two guarded indoor lots at either end of the station.

A fun day to peddle a bike is the annual Autovrije Zondag (Autofree Sunday; *www.autovrijezondag. nl*). It takes place in mid- to late September, and even though cab drivers are still allowed to drive like idiots through the city, a good portion of the Centrum is closed to motorized traffic.

Mike's Bike Tours - Kerkstraat 134, ☎ 622-7970
www.mikesbiketoursamsterdam.com

Slightly nervous about biking here for the first time? Want to learn colorful city history? Enjoy the comfort and sociability of riding with a group? Consider a guided bicycle tour with this reputable company. Mike's Bike's popular four-hour tour winds through the city and out into the countryside, including numerous stops and photo-ops along the way—like a windmill, a cheese farm, and other points of interest. The guides are knowl-edgeable about history and architecture but also about nightlife, urban lore, and where to party. The cost is €22 (€19 for students, €15 for kids). They also offer a city tour highlighting various neighborhoods, landmarks and hot spots for €19, €16 for students. It's a good deal. Reservations aren't necessary—just show up at Mike's Bike shop on Kerkstraat just off Leidsestraat. Departure times for the tours are daily as follows: March 1 to November 30, 11:00 country and 12:00 city. A winter tour also departs seven days a week at noon. Finally, if you want to peddle off on your own, Mike's has the coolest-looking rental bikes in town. They cost €8 for a day rental and €12 for 24 hours (optional insurance €3 per day; photo ID, a credit card, or €200 cash deposit required). They also offer great discounts for multiple day rentals. Open: Daily (Mar-Nov) 9-18; (Dec-Feb) 10-18. Closed on Queen's Day. (Map area C7)

Macbike - Centraal Station, ☎ 625-3845; Mr. Visserplein 2, ☎ 620-0985;
Marnixstraat 220, ☎ 626-6964; Weteringschans 2 (by Leidseplein), ☎ 528-7688

www.macbike.nl

Macbike has quality bikes and a good reputation, but sometimes there are long lines to pick up and re-turn rentals. And the bikes have big, annoying signs on the front that scream "tourist." Standard bikes cost €9.50 per day (24 hours). Bikes with handbrakes and gears cost €14.25 per business day. The more days you rent, the cheaper it gets. A €50 deposit or a credit card slip, plus a passport, is required. Optional theft insurance costs €3 per day. They also sell maps and information on cycling routes in and outside the city. Open: Daily 9-17:45. (Map areas B5, E6, C7, B7)

Rent A Bike Damstraat - Damstraat 20, ☎ 625-5029

www.bikes.nl

You'll find tourist friendly Rent A Bike in an alley off Damstraat just east of Dam Square. Their bikes have big ads attached to the front carriers—the only drawback to renting here. You can rent by the hour (€3.50 for the first hour, then cheaper for each additional hour), or by the day (€9.50 for 24 hours). Their special weekly rate is €35.25. They require a €25 deposit (cash or credit card) and a passport. Seats and helmets for kids are also available. Keep your eyes peeled for their small coupons that are worth a 10-25% discount. Open: Daily 9-18. (Map area D5)

Frederic Rent a Bike - Brouwersgracht 78, ☎ 624-5509

www.frederic.nl

It's just a 10-minute walk from Centraal Station to this small shop. They charge €10 a day (24 hours) and the price includes insurance and a child-seat if you need it. They don't ask for a deposit, just a credit card or passport. And there's no advertising on their bikes, which is a nice touch. They also organize room rentals in several houses and boats in the neighborhood and the prices are pretty good. Open Daily 9-18. (Map area D3)

Recycled Bicycles - Spuistraat 84A, ☎ 06-5468-1429

www.recycledbicycles.org

This hole-in-the wall bike shop is one of the smallest, coolest and definitely the cheapest in Amsterdam. The owner of this little company used to build bikes from spare parts that were donated or garbage-picked, but the Dutch cops eventually stopped his business by claiming everything found in the garbage – including junked bicycles – is property of the Queen! What a bunch of shit! Luckily, he still sells used and rebuilt bikes at fantastic prices and none of them are stolen. You can usually pedal away for between €40 and €65 (and that includes a one-month guarantee). This is an inexpensive alternative if you plan to stay in Amsterdam for an extended period, plus they let you sell your bike back to the shop when you leave. Rentals are €5 a day with a €50 cash deposit—that's extremely cheap. Mon-Fri 9-18 (siesta from 12-1); Sat 14-18. (Map area D4)

Markplaats

www.markplaats.nl

If your sojourn to Amsterdam turns into an extended stay (it happens), consider buying a bicycle online. This is the Dutch version of Ebay with pages of used bike listings. Another alternative site is *www tweedehands.nl* .

Soul Cycle - Nieuwe Herengracht 33, ☎ 771-5484

www.soulcycle.nl

Though there's sometimes rivalry with the skateboarders, most of the spots mentioned for skateboarding in the Hanging Out chapter get used by BMX riders too. Check out this shop to get the most up-to-date info on what's really happening in the scene – they know what's up. (Map area E6)

Tall Bikes

www.tallbike.net

Original tall bike constructor and guru, the legendary squat inventor Moonflyer, has sadly passed on, but his legacy remains. These custom-made super-tall bikes are designed and created for a variety of purposes, including jousting tournaments. That's right, jousting! They're quite an impressive spectacle. The website has pics and info about other events, too, including the Bike Wars demolition derby where, with some heavy tunes playing in the background, participants ride around and smash the crap out of each other's bikes until only one is still rideable. Cool.

Critical Ass - Mid-June

www.worldnakedbikeride.org

Why would a horde of cyclists meet annually to ride naked through the streets of Amsterdam? According to the organizers of the World Naked Bike Ride, it's to "protest against indecent exposure to automobile emissions and to celebrate the power and individuality of our bodies." In the past, the meeting point has been at Centraal Station.

Inline skating

Friday Night Skate - Vondelpark

www.fridaynightskate.nl

As long as the roads are dry, skaters (inline and roller) meet every Friday evening at 20:00 just to the right of Café Vertigo in Vondelpark and head out for a 15-kilometer tour through the city. Everyone is welcome, but you should be an experienced skater. (Map area B8)

Electric mopeds and Segways

Electric mopeds and Segways are two alternative ways to cruise around Amsterdam. Solex Tours (Brouwersgracht 163, *www.solextoursamsterdam.nl*) has moped rentals and guided tours. Amsterdam Segway, located just east of Centraal Station near the cruiseship terminal (Piet Heinkade 25, *www.segway.nl*) has these awesome stand up people movers for rent or for city tours.

Public Transport

Most people visiting Amsterdam stay mainly in the center and don't have to rely too much on public transit. But if you need it, you'll find there's a good network of trams, buses and Metro (subway) lines.

All Amsterdam public transportation now runs on a card system called the OV-chip card. You can "top up" the cards with as much tram, bus and Metro travel time you may wish to purchase (anywhere from 24 to168 hours, good across all forms of public transportation). The cards are available for cash purchase only at Centraal Station and at the entrances to several supermarkets. For the short term you can also buy a one-hour unlimited travel card on board trams and buses for €2,60, a premium price but more convenient than the OV-chip card.

To request a stop, push a red button on one of the poles (the Metro makes each stop automatically). To disembark, push the button by the door. Be sure to check in and out with your OV-chip card upon entering and exiting or your card will be charged €4 extra each time.

getting around

In addition to the regular buses and trams, Amsterdam also has a mini-bus service called the Stop/Go that leaves Centraal Station every 10 minutes, runs along the Brouwersgracht, Prinsengracht, Amstel, and ends at the Stopera (see Free Concerts, Hanging Out chapter) where the Waterlooplein flea market is. There are no stops: you can flag it down and get on or off anywhere along the route. It costs €1 for a one-hour ticket and you can also use OV-chip cards. (Hours of service, Mon-Sat 7:30-18:30.)

For more information about public transit (or help finding your way somewhere), visit the GVB ticket office and pick up a free route map. Walk across the little square in front of Centraal Station and you'll see it on your left, in the same building as the Tourist Office. (Open: Mon-Fri 7-21; Sat-Sun 8-21.) You can also call 0900-9292 for directions, but it costs 70 cents per minute and I've found that they often give bad advice. Perhaps it's a feeble attempt to get people to support the privatization of public transit.

Since I'm complaining, I'll tell you another thing that's fucked in Amsterdam: the big construction messes that you'll encounter all over the city for the next half-decade or so are the result of work on a "North/South" subway line. It's one of those extremely unpopular, ill-conceived mega-projects that take many years to complete and steadily leech millions of euros from education and other social services. You know, the kind of project that stays alive in spite of safety concerns, serious doubts about its necessity, and ongoing allegations of massive fraud.

cars

Parking

There are already too many fucking cars in Amsterdam, but if you have to drive into the city the best thing to do is put your car in a garage--and leave it there. It's expensive but nowhere near as much as if you get caught parking illegally. The Arena/Transferium (tel: 400-1721) is a huge garage under the Arena stadium south of the city center (from the A10 take exit A9/A2 and turn off at Ouderkerk aan de Amstel). It's one of several Park-and-Ride lots located around the outskirts of the city. Their normal price is €19 a day, but they have a special deal: 24 hour parking and 2 free public transport tickets for only €5.50. Take your parking ticket to the P+R kiosk and they'll give you the free tickets and explain how the discount works. Innercity parking is much more expensive. At the Heinekenplein lot (entrance off Eerste van der Helststraat, 470-0888), the price is €2.50 an hour (€25 a day). They're open Mon-Sat from 7:30 to 2:00 (Map area D8). ANVB Parking (Prins Hendrikkade 20a, 638-5330) costs even more – €3.40/hour; €42.50/day – but it's open 24 hours (Map area D3). For a list of all the parking garages in Amsterdam, along with maps and prices, check online at: *www.naaramsterdam.nl*

From 9 until midnight (noon to midnight on Sundays), parking in the center costs about €4 an hour and the prices are constantly rising. Amsterdam Centrum is now one of the most expensive places for parking in the world – four times as much as Paris! You pay at little blue boxes that are on every block, and the instructions are in English. The further out you go, the cheaper the price. A day ticket (from 9 to 19:00) in Osdorp and the western part of Bos en Lommer costs €6.60. Don't fuck around to save a couple of euros – the parking police work on quotas and they can spot an out-of-town plate or a rental car from a kilometer away. If you get ticketed, towed or the dreaded wheel clamp you'll be out serious money.

Car Rental

If you want to rent a car, look in the Yellow Pages under *Autoverhuur*. Kuperus has small cars starting at €25 per day in the east end (Van der Madeweg 1, 668 3311), but the guys who work there are exceedingly unpleasant: it might be worth it to pay a bit more somewhere else. I once got a good deal from Sixt (Amsteldijk 52; 470 8883). Avoid Adams Rent a Car Service and Ouke Baas. Note that if you can provide an Amsterdam address for the rental agreement, you might get a better deal from the major rental companies as some have special rates for residents.

24-Hour Gas Stations

There are gas stations open 24 hours at Sarphatistraat 225 and Marnixstraat 250. Try and avoid Shell when you're buying gas. Shell Oil (Dutch Royal Shell) helped prop up the apartheid regime in South Africa. They also supported the corrupt military dictatorship in Nigeria that murdered Ken Saro-Wiwa, an Ogoni poet who publicly protested Shell's environmentally catastrophic, outdated oil pumping techniques. Shell isn't the only sleazy oil company around, but they are the target of a world-wide boycott. Hit the greedy bastards where it hurts them the most: in their pockets.

Taxis

www.taxi.amsterdam.nl

They're expensive, and they treat cyclists like shit, but if you really need one call 777-7777 and enjoy the service: these taxis are very comfortable. You can sometimes flag one down on the street, but usually you have to go to a taxi stand. You'll find them at Centraal Station, Dam Square, Leidseplein, Rembrandtplein, Nieuwmarkt, Haarlemmerpoort, the Tropenmuseum…. Note: if you're treated badly by a driver, or think that you might have been overcharged, be sure to get a receipt, jot down the license plate number, the exact time of the journey, and then call this Complaint Line: 0900-202-1881 (13 cents a minute).

Bicycle Taxis

www.wielertaxi.nl

You'll find bike taxis all over the center and at their home base, Dam square. They're a bit expensive, but can be a nice way to kick back and tour old Amsterdam. You can also reserve door to door rides on their website.

Tuk Tuk Company

www.tuktukcompany.nl

Two people can ride in a Thai-style Tuk Tuk taxi, a three-wheeled scooter with back seats, anywhere within Amsterdam's center ring for €3 per person, Friday and Saturday nights from 22-3. If you're out partying this is a great way to travel, much cheaper than standard taxis. Their stations are at Leidseplein, Albert Cuyp Markt and Amstel Station.

boats

Tours

Boat tours leave from several docks in front of Centraal Station and along the Damrak and Rokin. It's very touristy, but it's fun to see the city from the canal perspective, and some of the taped info is interesting. The tours usually give you a quick look at the harbor and then cruise along the canals while a recording describes the sights in four languages. The one-hour routes vary slightly and depart every 20 minutes or so. Amsterdam canals are particularly beautiful at night. The last tours depart at 22:00 and are often sold out in advance during high season.

getting around

St. Nicolaas Boat Club
www.amsterdamboatclub.com

While the tours above are okay, these trips are way more fun. '30s-era flat-bottomed boats, perfect for criusing canals the big tour boats can't navigate, make this non-profit club unique. Ten people fit aboard and there's plenty of space for food and drinks (which you bring yourself.) Smoking weed isn't a problem either. The sociable captains will gladly answer questions and they know all kinds of cool stories about places along the routes. There are several tours a day and sometimes at night. More info and tour sign up at Mike's Bikes, Kerkstraat 134. There's a suggested donation of €10. (Map area C7)

ferries

Behind Centraal Station you'll find free ferries for the brief journey to North Amsterdam departing every few minutes. If you're on a bike, it's a good starting point for a peddle into the countryside. Most of the bike-rental places will give you free info about scenic routes. There's also a ferry to the NDSM terrain that takes about 10 minutes (see Music, Hanging Out).

Canal Motorboats - Zandhoek 10A, ☎ 422-7007

www.canalmotorboats.com

Six passenger electric-powered boats are available here. After a short introductory lesson, you're free to putt around the city's famous canals. The rentals cost €50 for the first hour, €40 for the second and €30 for the third. Additional hours cost €20 each. An ID and €150 or a credit card is needed for a deposit. It's a bit expensive, but it's not too bad if you're with a group, and you'll have a unique experience being your own skipper. Bring a picnic and munch away as you cruise Amsterdam's historic canals. Located just north of Haarlemmerdijk/Prinsengracht corner, on the Westerdok. (Map area C1)

Rent A Boat Amsterdam - Nassaukade Marina, ☎ 624-7635

www.rentaboatamsterdam.com

Beautiful, six person, Amsterdam style sloep boats are available from this online company. Reservations can only be made online. They require a €150 deposit, then the boats are €50 per hour. Check out their website for more details. (Map area B3)

Canal Bikes - ☎ 626-5574

www.canal.nl

Two-to-four-person pedal boats called Canal Bikes are all over the old city canals in summer and are a lot of fun. They can be rented at several locations, including in front of the Rijksmuseum, near Leidseplein, and Anne Frank House. One or two people pay €8 per hour each; 3 or more people pay €7 per hour each. Deposit: €20 per boat. Open: in summer 10-18 ('til 22 if the weather is really nice) and in winter, only at the dock opposite the Rijksmuseum, 10-18.

a note on bike thief motherfuckers

Last year in Amsterdam over 100,000 bikes were stolen. Sorry-looking dope fiends who cruise around mumbling "*fiets te koop*" sell hot bikes, but more are actually stolen by organised gangs. Junkies sell the bikes cheap, but if you're tempted to buy one while you're here, think again. When you buy a stolen bike you're hurting the person who owned it, as well as keeping the asshole who nicked it in business. You can also get busted: The cops are cracking down on bike theft by arresting people when they buy a stolen bicycle. Supporting shops like Recycled Bicycles, where 2nd-handers are sold cheap but legal and in perfect working order, flies the finger to all the pathetic fuckers hocking stolen bikes for profit or to pay for their habits.

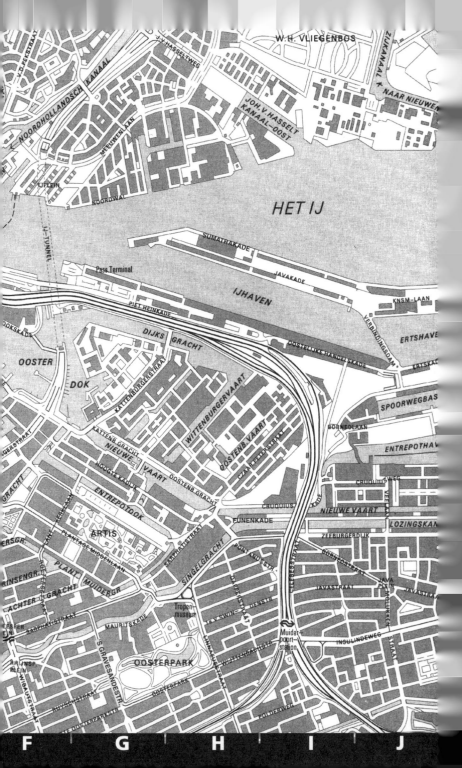

W.H. VLIEGENBOS

ZIJKANAAL K. NAAR NIEUWE

K. NOORDHOLLANDSCH KANAAL

J.V. HASSELTWEG

JOH. V. HASSELT KANAAL—OOST

MEEUWENLAAN

IJPLEIN

NOORDWAL

J.TUNNEL

HET IJ

SUMATRAKADE

Pass.Terminal

JAVAKADE

IJHAVEN

KNSM—LAAN

PIET HEINKADE

VERBINDINGSDAM

OOKSKADE

DIJKS GRACHT

OOSTELIJKE HANDELSKADE

ERTSHAVE

OOSTER

ERTSKA

DOK

KATTENBURGERSTRAAT

SPOORWEGBAS

WITTENBURGERVAART

BORNEOLAAN

ERSTRAAT

KATTENB.GRACHT

NIEUWE VAART

OOSTENB.VAART

ENTREPOTHAV

HOOGTE KADIJK

OOSTENB.GRACHT

CZAAR PETERSTRAAT

CRUQUIUSWEG

GRACHT

ENTREPOTDOK

CRUQUIUS KADE

NIEUWE VAART

LOZINGSKAN

ARTIS

SARPHATISTRAAT

FUNENKADE

ZEEBURGERDIJK

ERSGH.

PLANTAGE MIDDENLAAN

BORNEOSTRAAT

PLANT MUIDERGR

PONT ANJE STR.

JAVASTRAAT

JAVA PLEIN

JAVASTRAAT

RINSENGR

P.V. GEESTSTRAAT

J. MOLUKKEN STR.

ACHTER GRACHT

BLANKENSTR.

EERSTE EN

SARPHATISTRAAT

J.V. SWIN DENSTR.

RH. JNSP PLEIN

MAURITSKADE

Tropen-museum

INSULINDEWEG

S GRAVESANDESTR

Muider-poort-station

WIBAUTSTR.

OOSTERPARK

OOSTERPARK

RUYSCHSTRAAT

MIDDENLAAN

POLDERWEG

1E OOSTERPARKSTR.

OOSTERPARKSTR.

F   G   H   I   J

Getting out of Amsterdam

train

Train travel is certainly the most pleasant and comfortable way to get around Europe, but it can also be expensive. The Dutch system in particular has seen massive price hikes in recent years and major cuts in service. On some routes you have to reserve a seat (and pay a reservation fee) even if the train isn't full, which seems kind of ludicrous. But in the summertime it's a good idea to book a seat even when it isn't mandatory. The booking office for international train journeys is at the front of the station, left of the main entrance. Grab a number and be prepared to wait. Tickets for destinations within Holland can also be purchased here or from the big yellow machines (which have instructions in English). If you buy your tickets from a person, there's an additional 50-cents-per-ticket service charge, and – note well – neither the ticket office nor the machines take credit cards. For international train info and reservations by phone, call 0900-9296 (35 cents/min plus €3.50 per ticket service charge); for trains within the Netherlands, dial 0900-9292 (70 cents/min). Online, go to: *www.ns.nl*. The website also provides information about special deals on rail travel in Holland.

Thalys - ☎ 0900-9296 (35 cents/min)

www.thalys.com

Here's a tip: If you're planning to go from Amsterdam to Paris, you can ride this high-speed train from Centraal Station to Gare du Nord for around €80 round-trip. It's a little more expensive than the bus but takes about half the time (4 hours) and it's much more comfortable. There are only a few seats offered at this price on each train, so book early.

bus

Eurolines - Rokin 10; Amstel Station, ☎ 560-8788

www.eurolines.n

Eurolines has service to almost 500 destinations. I've had both good and bad experiences with this company, from making new friends toting a bottle of booze, to being forcibly locked out of the bus for a long hour in front of the freezing and sleazy Hamburg bus station, but they are much cheaper than the train, especially off-season. Check it out early because not all routes are served daily and they often sell out in advance. You need to provide your passport number to buy a ticket. Keep in mind that border checks, especially going into France, tend to be a lot more severe on buses than on other modes of transport. Rokin office open: Mon-Fri 9:30-17:30; Sat 11-16. Amstel Station office open: Daily 7-22:30 (Map area D5)

hitching

There is a lot of competition hitchhiking out of Amsterdam in the summer, but people do give lifts. Hitching isn't allowed on the national highways: stay on the on-ramps or in gas stations. It's easier for drivers or truckers to pick you up and you'll avoid hassles from the cops. I once caught a ride at a gas station all the way to Munich with an herb smoking German trucker. If you're heading to Utrecht, take tram 25 to the end of the line and join the crowd on the Utrechtseweg. How about southern or central Germany? Hop the metro to Amstel station and try your luck on the Gooiseweg. For Rotterdam and The Hague go by tram 4 to the RAI convention centre and walk down Europaboulevard until you see the entrance to the A2 highway. But before you hit the road, check *www.hitchhikers.org* and see if you can arrange a ride without breathing exhaust. Good luck.

air travel

Budget Travel Agencies

There are a couple of budget travel agencies south of Dam Square (going away from Centraal Station). Budget Air is at Rokin 34 (627-1251). For last-minute specials (mostly to southern Europe and North Africa) check the L'tur site (320-5783; *www.ltur ams.com*), or visit their counter at Schiphol Airport. Martinair also has a counter at Schiphol Airport (601-1767; *www.martinair.com*) where tickets for last-minute flights can be purchased. I had a good experience once at D reizen (Ferdinand Bolstraat 58; 200-1672), which is part of a big chain. They've got last-minute deals on various airlines for two people travelling together. World Ticket Center (Nieuwezijds Voorburgwal 159, 626-1011) sometimes has special offers and the consultants there are very nice. Note that all travel agencies in Amsterdam tack on an exorbitant "service charge" of about €15 per person! For a complete listing of travel agencies, look in the phone book (the white pages) under *Reisbureau*. Shop around.

easyJet

www.easyjet.com

Like most airlines, they suck. But at least easyJet isn't so expensive. Book online with a credit card and you can get some dirt-cheap fares. You can fly one-way from Amsterdam, including all taxes, to London for €42, Geneva for €50, and Mallorca for €37! They fly to several other destinations as well. There's no paper ticket: just print your confirmation and bring it to the airport.

Transavia

www.transavia.com

Transavia is a Dutch airline offering cheap flights from Amsterdam to dozens of European destinations as well as Egypt, Turkey and Morocco.

Jet2

www.jet2.com

This little airline has one-way no-frills flights from Amsterdam to Manchester for only €14, but tax is another €28. Thomson (*www.thomsonfly.com*) also has cheap flights to England, and I once flew from London to Amsterdam on BMI (*www.flybmi.com*) for €10 plus tax. In fact, BMI is about as good as it gets in this category.

Snowflake

www.flysnowflake.com

SAS operates this budget airline. They fly one way to Copenhagen for €78 including all taxes.

KLM

www.klm.com

The official Dutch airline sometimes offers pretty good fares, both one-way and return. They hit you up for an extra €10 for online bookings, but that's better than the €25 to €35 they charge you to do it by phone!

train to the airport

Easy as pie! Hop on the train at Centraal Station (€3.40) and you're at Schiphol Airport (*www.schiphol.nl*) in about 20 minutes. Trains depart regularly starting at about 4:40 in the morning until just after midnight. After that, there's just one train per hour. Keep a close eye on your luggage. (Did you know that Schiphol Airport is five meters below sea level?)

taxi to the airport

Taxi to Trust (489-6200) charges €30 to and from the city center. You can call them when you land at Schiphol, for instance, and they'll pick you up in 10 minutes. The TCA taxi company (677-7777) offers a set price (*vaste tarief*) from the center of Amsterdam to the airport. Currently the rate is €38. Make sure that you specify that you want that *vaste tarief* (pronounced "fast-ah teh-reef") when you book the cab on the phone, and again with the driver before he departs. Not all taxis will honor this rate from Schiphol into town. If the first cabbie in line refuses, continue until you find one who says yes – and you will. For more taxi info see the Getting Around chapter.

maps and travel books

à la Carte - Utrechtsestraat 110 112, ☎ 625-0679

Open: Mon 13-18; Tues-Fri 10-18 (in summer, Thurs 'til 21); Sat 10-17. (Map area E7)

Pied à Terre - Overtoom 135-137, ☎ 627-4455

www.piedaterre.nl

Open: Mon 13-18; Tues-Fri 11-18 (Thurs 'til 21; Sat 10-17.) (Map area C5)

Boekhandel Jacob van Wijngaarden - Overtoom 97, ☎ 612-1901

www.jvw.nl

Open: Mon 13-18; Tues-Fri 10-18 (Thurs 'til 21); Sat 10-17. (Map area A7)

Evenaar - Singel 348, ☎ 624-6289

http://travel.to/evenaar

(See Books & Magazines, Shopping chapter) Open: Mon-Fri 12-18; Sat 11-17. (Map area C5)

Practical shit

tourist info

The Amsterdam Tourist Office (a.k.a. the VVV) is the city's official tourist agency. However, it's also a privately-run business, so even though the people working here are almost always patient, friendly and helpful, you can see that their motivation is "sell, sell, sell." There's a branch inside Centraal Station, upstairs on platform 2b that's open Mon-Sat 8-20; Sun 9-17, and another just to the left as you cross the square in front of the station that's open daily from 9-17. There's also a branch at Leidseplein (open: Sun-Thurs 9:15-17; Fri-Sat 9:15-19). If you're here during high season, be prepared for a long wait. They have an info number (0900-400-4040; Mon-Fri 9-17), but at 40 cents per minute – including all the time you spend on hold – it's very expensive. (Map area E3)

money

While there may be valid arguments for a single European currency, the old white guys in suits that concocted this deal didn't do it for the benefit of you and me. The euro (€) is the official currency in the Netherlands. You don't have to change money now when you travel between most EU member countries, but you pay higher prices for everything.

As for banks, fuck them! They charge ridiculously high fees for changing money. However, changing money at bank alternatives in the tourist areas (like Leidseplein) is mostly a big rip-off, too: high commission charges and low exchange rates. Beware of places that advertise "no commission" in big letters followed by fine print that says "if you're purchasing" (this means if you're giving them euros to buy US $, for example). It's a scam, and once they have your money inside their bulletproof glass booth, you won't get it back. It's hard to recommend a place because they're changing all the time, but here are a few stable money changers.

practical shit

Lorentz Change - Damrak 31, ☎ 422-6002

www.lorentzchange.com

These guys offer the best rates on cash and no commission on non-euro currencies. Open: Daily, 24 hours. (Map area D4)

Pott Change - Damrak 95, ☎ 626-3658; Rembrandtplein 10, ☎ 626-8768

If you're changing non-euro currencies there's no commission charged here either, and Pott's fee for cashing non-euro travellers checks is relatively low. Open: Mon-Sat 8:15-20; Sun 9:15-20. (Map area D4)

American Express - Damrak 66, ☎ 504-8777

Amex doesn't charge a fee to process their own travellers' checks if you want them cashed out in euros. Open: Mon-Fri 9-17; Sat 9-12. (Map area D4)

GWK Bank - Centraal Station, ☎ 627-2731

This member of the bank mafia charges 1.5% commission on the total cash amount changed, plus an extra €2.25. And the fee for changing travellers' checks is even more. It's a rip-off but they're open late if you are stuck. Open: Mon-Sat 8-22; Sun 9-22. (Map area E3)

phone

Pay phones that take coins are almost extinct, and to use one of the few remaining phone booths—mostly found in train stations—you'll need a phone card. They can be purchased in denominations of €5 and €10 at the Tourist Office, post offices, tobacco shops and supermarkets. Phone booths have instructions in English.

For long distance calls dial 00, then your country code and the number. Holland's country code is 31. Amsterdam's city code is 20 from abroad and 020 if you're dialing from elsewhere in The Netherlands. Long-distance phone cards are available in most of the "call centers" on tourist strips like the Damrak, and at tobacco shops. They come in different denominations and they can be a very good deal. A card called EuroCity is a great buy. Easy-to-use instructions, in English, are printed on the back of the cards.

post

The Dutch postal service has been privatized, which has led to higher prices and the closure of hundreds of offices all over Holland. There are now only a few outlets left in Amsterdam's city center and they're always crowded. The main post office is located at Singel 250 (556-3311), at the corner of Raadhuisstraat, just west of Dam Square. Letters and postcards up to 20 grams cost 72 cents for Europe and 89 cents overseas. The main post office is open: Mon-Fri 9-18; Sat 10-13:30 (Map area C4)

The entrance to the Poste Restante is in the same building. If you're having mail sent to you the address is: Poste Restante, Hoofdpostkantoor TNT, Singel 250, 1012 SJ, Amsterdam, The Netherlands. Don't forget to bring your passport when you go to pick up your letters. Open: Mon-Fri 9-18:30; Sat 9-12.

Some supermarkets also sell stamps from vending machines near their entrances. For more postal info, call the free customer service line: 058-233-3333 (choose "9" twice to speak to a human).

If you're posting letters from a mailbox, the right-hand slot is for Amsterdam, and the left side is for the rest of the world.

If you want to send or receive e-mail, stop by an internet café or the main library. (see Hanging Out chapter). Got a laptop? There are many cafés, coffeeshops and bars with WiFi and they usually have stickers advertising this fact on the window.

left luggage

Lockers at Centraal Station cost about €4-5 for 24 hours. Bags are x-rayed before you can enter, and the area is closed at night from 1 to 7:00. Warning: Like all big train stations the world over, Centraal Station has its share of bag-snatchers. Never take your eyes off your luggage – not even for a second.

voltage

The Dutch electric current operates on 220 volts. If you're from Canada or the U.S. and you want to plug in something you've brought with you, get a converter and/or a transformer. It's probably cheaper to buy them in North America than Amsterdam.

weather

Expect lousy weather. Then if it's warm and dry you'll feel really lucky (which you will be). Bring layers of clothing and something waterproof. Umbrellas don't always do the trick, as this is a very windy country, especially in the fall. The North Sea wind also means that the weather can change very quickly, and even several times a day. Winters are cold, but it rarely goes much below freezing. July and August are your best bet for nice weather (of course) but not usually what one would call "summery." Having said all that, Amsterdam is a fun city to visit any time of year.

drinking water

Amsterdam boasts some of the cleanest drinking water of any European city so don't waste your money on absurdly expensive bottled water while wandering. Buy one then refill it! Every tap in this city is safe, from hotel room to men's room. Bars typically give glasses of water gratis. Restaurants, normally selling small H2O bottles for a couple of euros, will usually give you tap water if you ask for it. If they refuse, consider going elsewhere—there are plenty of friendly establishments in this city.

tipping

Tipping isn't really part of Dutch culture: Service is supposed to be included in the price at restaurants and cafés. But if you have a nice server you can round up the bill: 5% is sufficient; 10% is generous. At bars you can round up a bit, but it's not necessary. A little tip, however, can go a long way—guaranteeing prompt service for your next round. And if you don't have much dough, it's perfectly acceptable not to tip at all.

toilets

You often have to pay to use public toilets in Europe. There's usually an attendant on duty who's supposed to keep things clean and collects the 25 or 50 cents required. It's not a lot of money, but it sure does piss me off (excuse the pun). Expensive hotels are good places to find free, clean toilets. Just walk in looking confident and head straight in past the reception desk. There's always a washroom nearby. (I like The Grand at Oudezijds Voorburgwal 197). Also, if you can handle it, you can take a whiz for free in any police station. And guys should think twice before peeing in the canals or alleys: Not only are you acting like a pig, but you're risking around a €90 fine if a cop spots and accosts you.

free english news

Free arts and culture weekly newspapers (R.I.P. Amsterdam Weekly) are currently no longer publishing. Check *www.underwateramsterdam.com* for online weekly listings of all things cultural and cool.

The Amsterdam Times
www.theamsterdamtimes.nl

Currently Amsterdam's only free English paper, the Times covers mostly Dutch news and politics. It's published every Friday and can be found at Waterstones and the American Book Center in the Spui (see Shopping chapter).

Expatica
www.expatica.com

Though it's often geared towards the interests of corporate expats, this is a useful site for foreigners living in Holland. Along with features and listings, there are daily English summaries of current Dutch news items.

recycling

Bring used batteries to any supermarket. Toss them into the battery logoed box near the entrance. Glass and paper recycling bins (marked *glasbak* and *papierbak*) are found on street corners every few blocks.

laundry

The Wash Company - Haarlemmerdijk 132, ☎ 625-3672

Wash €5; dry (only in combo with wash) 20 cents per 6 minutes. Wash/dry/fold service takes 4 hours and costs €7 for 6kg. Open: Mon-Sat 8:45-19; Sun 10-19. (Map area C2)

Wash & Mail - Amstel 30

Wash €5 including soap; drying costs about €1.50. Internet access is €3 an hour. Wash and dry service is €8.50 and includes 15 minutes online or free coffee. Open: Daily 9:30-20. (Map area D6)

Wash-o-matic - Pieter Langendijk 12

Out near Vondelpark you can do a load of up to 8kg for €5. Dryers cost 20 cents for 6 minutes. Open: Daily 8-20 (last wash in at 19:00).

identification laws

Amsterdam is known for its tolerant culture. Being stopped and I.D.ed on the street was rare—one never feared police harassment. Unfortunately, this has changed—the pass laws are back, no longer a hideous historical anomaly, but a current issue. Everyone is now required by law to carry state-sanctioned identification with them at all times, ordinary people are routinely being checked and punished for non-compliance. This is just one of many regressive social changes that the now right-wing Dutch government has instituted. Outrage to this draconian law has been surprisingly muted but the Dutch folks who resist are creative and inspiring. For instance, one activist group (www.geen-id.nl) encourages people to not carry ID and created an insurance fund covering fines and bail. While it's unlikely you'll be stopped, be aware of this offensive law. Personally, as an avid traveller, I believe the safest passport stash place is a hotel safe.

pickpockets

Amsterdam is a safe city, the only crime you may witness or experience is pickpocketing. Watch out for these assholes: they're extremely clever. Keep your valuables safely stashed and watch your bags at all times. The worst areas are around Centraal Station, Dam Square, Leidseplein, and the Red Light District –tourist areas where most travellers end up at least a couple of times during their visit. These thieves also work on public transit and the trains (especially to and from Schiphol airport). Try not to act like a total space cadet (in spite of how you might feel) and you probably won't have any problems. If you do, see the Phone Numbers chapter for help you'll need.

drug testing

Hard drugs are illegal in Holland. Buying them from strangers can be dangerous--anything bought on the street is guaranteed to be crap. But if you've scored some ecstasy or coke elsewhere and want to be sure it's okay, drop in at the Stichting Adviesburo Drugs (Entrepotdok 32a, 623-7943; www.adviesburodrugs.nl). They do not sell drugs--it's a non-profit foundation that, among other things, will test your ecstasy and tell you exactly what it is. They take a tiny sample and usually have the results within a couple of minutes. This is a fantastic service (anonymous too.) By testing and cross-referencing they can track the market and get bunk or unclean drugs out of circulation. Open: Tues-Fri 14-17 (Thurs 'til 19:30). (Map Area G6)

smoking ban

The Netherlands, one of the last bastions of cigarette smoking in Europe, finally decreed in 2008 that tobacco must be banned completely from public places. This means you can enjoy a meal in a tiny café without the blue haze that used to be so common. Bars and clubs are trying to keep their patrons happy while having to send them outside, sometimes in the cold and rain, to puff smokes. Some bars have ignored the scarcely-enforced ban, especially late at night, or have big customer contribution jars to pay off possible fines. A handful of bars and coffeeshops have separate smoking rooms, but many people are taking their cigarettes and joints outside. Here's the coolest and craziest part: Pure weed can still be smoked in coffeeshops. The Dutch health minister claims that cannabis, unlike tobacco, hasn't proved to be harmful to your health. That's some seriously progressive thinking!

Most coffeeshops have banned mixed spliffs (rolled with tobacco, European-style) and insist that their patrons smoke pure joints, while some don't seem to mind. Several shops have a herbal tobacco substitute which looks like tea–you can also brew it, and apparently smells like a burning Christmas tree. I don't know anybody who uses it, but it's available. You can also smoke joints in certain bars, like Batavia, Barney's Uptown and Kashmir Lounge (see Bars chapter.)

In clubs like the Paradiso small smoking rooms are provided, but the effect is a bit claustrophobic, like in a smoky airport box. Concerts, especially in small, crowded halls, now tend to smell like sweat and beer instead of cigarettes. I personally think clubs need to hire aroma jockeys (like Amsterdam's own Odo 7, www.odo7.com) to mix smells with music – our noses will appreciate it!

gay and lesbian info

The Cool Guide has never included a lesbian and gay chapter. Instead, in each section of the book a couple of spots that cater mainly to a gay crowd are listed (and any place that isn't gay-friendly won't be listed at all). Find out more about gay Amsterdam happenings at the fabulous Pink Point kiosk on Westermarkt square (just in front of the Homomonument). They provide all sorts of free info including the *Gay News* and the *Lesbian Listings*. Pink Point also sells guidebooks (check out Darren Reynoldson's *The Bent Guide*) and a plethora of unique souvenirs. Open: daily 10-18 in summer; Fri-Mon 10-17 in winter. (Map area C4)

a note about squatting in Amsterdam

Squatting--or occupying empty buildings--became legal due to Amsterdam's severe housing shortage. This protected the city from speculators sitting on property waiting for rising real estate prices. Cheap or free housing and work spaces allowed a vibrant counter-culture of artists, students, musicians, mechanics, anarchists and misanthropes to shape Amsterdam's DIY bohemian lifestyle—with concert venues, radio stations, vegan cafés, political activism and pyrotechnic parties the result. Usually, this required hard labor from the occupants to make the spaces liveable. Recently, the new right-wing Dutch government has declared squatting illegal. Hundreds of Amsterdam based squats are in the process of being evicted.

Some buildings have been legalized and some squats have struck deals with the owners to remain, but the majority are in danger. The European Commission on Human Rights has meanwhile found the new law unfair to eastern European EU member citizens working in Amsterdam who can't find/afford housing and have squatted as an alternative. Some of them were evicted in freezing temperatures, with nowhere to go.

The Amsterdam squatting community sees the new law as ludicrous and plasters banners citywide reading *Kraken Gaat Door!*--which means Squatting Will Continue! Supporting the remaining squatted cafés, restaurants, bars and venues (many of which are in this book) says a big *Fuck You* to conservative pigs who care more about money than people. Check *http://squat.net* for squatting info or the excellent *http://radar.squat.net* for up to date listings.

Food

Eating out in Amsterdam can be expensive, particularly since the introduction of the euro several years ago. But pay attention to this chapter and I promise you a full belly at the best price. Don't be surprised if service in some restaurants is not particularly friendly, and don't take it personally: Rude isn't just a popular Dutch name.

If you're on a super-tight budget, head to the outdoor markets for the cheapest fruit, veggies and cheese. Several are listed in the Shopping chapter. For dry foods, go to the large supermarkets and remember to bring your own bags, otherwise you pay for the luxury of a plastic bag, here.

Got access to a kitchen? Try visiting a *tropische winkel* for inspiration. They're found throughout the city, especially near the markets, and they specialize in foods from tropical countries: everything from mangoes to hot sauce to cassava chips.

supermarkets

Amsterdam supermarkets are thankfully open longer than they used to be –until nine or ten o'clock at night. More stores are staying open on Sundays, too—a convenient trend. At some stores you weigh produce yourself. Push the button marked *"bon"* and a sticker with the price pops out of the scale. If there's no *"bon"* button on the scale, it means they'll price your veggies or fruit at the check-out. At Albert Heijn supermarkets pick up a free plastic *"bonus card"* if you want to buy an item on sale: without it you'll be charged the full price. Just ask for one at the front counter and hand it to the cashier when you pay.

Aldi - Nieuwe Weteringstraat 26; Admiraal de Ruijterweg 56C (West End)

   One of the cheapest, but their selection doesn't compare to the bigger chains. (Map areas C8, 5A)

Dirk van den Broek - Marie Heinekenplein; Bilderdijkstraat 26

   The best of the cheapies, and they stock organic products. The big American-style stores: behind the Heineken Brewery and at Bilderdijkstraat, Amsterdam West. (Map areas D8, 5A)

Albert Heijn

Nieuwezijds Voorburgwal behind Dam Square; Van Baerlestraat 33; Haarlemmerdijk 1; odenbreestraat 20; Koningsplein; Centraal Station

Every time I blink there's a new one. My friend calls them Adolf Heijn, because of the way they've conquered Holland and occupy every neighborhood. However, they carry lots of organic products (look for labels marked *bio*), and all the branches listed above stay open until 22:00 ('til 19 on sun), except the Haarlemmerdijk store closes at 21. The stores can be poorly stocked and also relatively expensive, but location and convenience are definitely their strong points. The Albert off of Dam Square and the Jodenbreestraat installation are both well stocked with a good selection, which is not so good at the Koningsplein store. The big Albert on Van Baerlestraat is at the far end of the Museumplein, while the Haarlemmerdijk store is only a 10-minute walk from Centraal Station. The smaller AH to go shops, like Centraal Station's in the west tunnel by Shakies are more expensive than the bigger stores but handy if you're catching a train—and this outlet is open daily 'til 22:00. (Map areas D5, B8, C3, E5, C6)

health food stores

De Natuurwinkel/Eko-Plaza

Elandsgracht 118, ☎ 412-4696; Haarlemmerdijk 162; Weteringschans 133; 1e Constantijn Huygensstraat 49; 1e van Swindenstraat 30

www.denatuurwinkel.nl www.ekoplaza.nl

Health food, supermarket style. They stock a good selection including organic produce, cheese and baked goods. If you buy fruit or vegetables here, look for the number next to each item, then punch in the number when you weigh the item. Next push the button marked bon and a sticker will come out with the price. It's less complicated than it sounds plus you won't be embarrassed at check-out when they send you back to the scale. There's a big, busy bulletin board by the front door at the Elandsgracht store: Open Mon-Sat 8-19; Sun 10-18. (Map area B5)

Marqt - Overtoom 21, Utrechtsestraat 17

www.marqt.nl

This grocery store chain is a novel edition to Amsterdam's organic and slow food movement, combining a stunning selection with a new payment premise—no cash. They'll gladly take your plastic, however. Warehouse chic décor at the Utrechtsestraat locale, simple floor plan and isles of scrumptious delectables—the chip/crisp isle alone is larger than many local health food stores. All the baked goods, breads, cakes, cookies, pizzas and chef prepared daily specials are created in house. Prices can be steep: premium sustainable wild Alaskan salmon €80 a kilo! But for deli treats, baked goods or picnic edibles, Marqt is a worthwhile stop. Marqt Utrechtsestraat Open: Mon-Sat 9-21; Sun 11-20 Overtoom Mon-Sat 9-20; Sun 10-19. (Map area D6)

Delicious Food - Westerstraat 24, ☎ 320-3070

www.deliciousfood.nl

If the smell of fresh-roasted coffee beans doesn't draw you into this inviting shop, then maybe one of the other 250 organic products on offer will. They have freshly baked breads and cakes, lots of bulk products (a relatively new thing here in the Netherlands), fresh produce and a good selection of wines. There's a small deli in the back for take-out. It's right by the Noordermarkt (see Markets, Shopping chapter). Open: Mon, Wed-Sat 10-19; Sun 11-15. (Map area C3) food

Organic - Cornelis Schuytstraat 26, ☎ 379-5195

www.organicfoodforyou.n

If you find yourself in this well-to-do neighborhood between Vondelpark and Museumplein, check ou this charming organic food store. They stock a wide range of fresh foods from meat and dairy products to bread, fruit, vegetables and more. It's all tastefully displayed along with information about the products origins and use. Organic is definitely upmarket, but decently priced take-away soups and sandwiches are available—handy if you're on your way to the park. Open: Mon-Fri 9-19; Sat 9-18. (Map area A8)

De Aanzet - Frans Halsstraat 27, ☎ 673-3415

This cooperatively run store is not far from the Albert Cuyp market (see Markets, Shopping chapter) They stock bulk products, organic fruits and veggies, and yummy baked goods. Open: Mon-Fri 9-18 Sat 9-17. (Map area C8)

Oase Natuurvoeding - Jan Pieter Heijestraat 105, ☎ 618-2887

If you're in Vondelpark and need some picnic fixin's, stop by this neighborhood health-food store.. And bring an empty bottle because they also have organic wine on tap! Open: Mon-Fri 8-18; Sat 8-17.

street foods

Falafel stands are scattered all about the city. **Maoz Falafel** (see Restaurants, below) are delicious and one of the best deals in town: You can stuff yourself for only €5. Burp!

The quality and origin of the meat is a little dubious, but for **shoarma** take-away try the Damstraa (just east of Dam Square), where there's a whole row of places to cop. **Ben Cohen** has high-quality Israeli-style veal shoarma at Rozengracht 239 (Map area B5) and is rated one of Amsterdam's best

For **french fries** (chips to you Brits) try any place that advertises vlaamse frites (Flemish fries). These are the best. There's a large choice of toppings-- get mayonnaise for the Dutch experience or Oorlog (half mayo half peanut sauce.) The best place, as evidenced by the long line-ups, is **Vleminckx** a Voetboogstraat 33, which runs parallel to the big walking street, the Kalverstraat. They're open daily until 18:00 (Thurs 'til 19). There's also **Mannequin Pis** at Damrak 42, near Centraal Station. And there's a pretty good one called **De Belg** (Reguliersbreestraat 49), near the Rembrandtplein. If you don't mind spending a bit more, you can get fries made from organic potatoes at **Morning Sta** (see Restaurants, below). Delicious.

Healthy fast food is a now a trend in Amsterdam, but **Shakies** (Centraal Station west tunnel 423-4377; and in Amstel Station, too) still rules the train stations. They make great juices and shakes—all the fruit is freshly squeezed and the milk and yoghurt are organic. If you're vegan o lactose-intolerant, they even have soya milk. Prices start at €2.95 and for an extra 70 cents they' throw in a shot of vitamin B, ginseng or guarana. Also on the menu are organic veggie samosas and seitan rolls, bagels with cream cheese and herbal teas, as well as options for vegans. Open Mon-Fri 7-21; Sat 8-20:30; Sun 9-20:30.

Het Kaasboertje (2e Tuindwarsstraat 3; 624-8802) is a small shop in the Jordaan neighborhood tha sells big, filling **sandwiches** at great prices (several are less than €2). The owner is super-friendly and he'll build whatever you want from their huge selection of cheeses, pates, fish, and meat Drinks are cheap, too. They only do take-out, but there's a small bench out front. **Lombardo's** (Nieuwe Spiegelstraat 50) serves fresh, high quality baguette and roll sandwiches (the salmon pate with seaweed salad and avocado is a killer!) Prices here are reasonable and all the food is prepared

n house. **Lookie** (Utrechtstraat 57) make superb sub style sandwiches. Choose from a mega menu or create your own!

Fish lovers should definitely try snacking at one of the herring stalls that are all over the city, easily recognizable by their fish flags. There's one close to Centraal Station on the bridge where the Haarlemmerstraat crosses the Singel canal and another next to the Westerkerk. All kinds of fish and seafood sandwiches are available.

Another good bet for cheap food is **Indonesian** or **Surinamese** take-away. A big roti meal will cost you about €6, as will a large plate of fried rice (nasi) or noodles (bami) with vegetables. The portions are often enough for two people. Add a couple of euros if you want it with chicken or pork. See Restaurants, below, for some suggestions.

For relatively cheap **Chinese** take-away look around the Zeedijk (above the Nieuwmarkt) where there's a small Chinatown. And at the outdoor markets don't forget to try the cheap and addictive **Vietnamese Loempias** (spring rolls): veggie or chicken, €1.

If you're looking for classy **picnic fixings**, stop by **Raïnaraï** (Prinsengracht 252; 624-9791; *www.raïnaraï.nl*), a Mediterranean catering and take-away shop specializing in "nomadic food." They use high-quality, mainly organic ingredients, so it's tasty but not super-cheap. Veggie couscous is €8; sandwiches are €5.50 and up; containers of hummus, mushroom pate or mackerel mousse are €2 to €3.50; and stuffed mushrooms go for €2. **Le Sud** has two locations: in the Centrum (Haarlemerdijk 118, map area C2) and near the Westerpark (Spaarndammerstraat 143, map area B1). Vegetarian Mediterranean/Persian food is their specialty, including several varieties of the best hummus in town plus sandwiches, salads, dolmas and lots more…perfect for a picnic in the park.

food

The bakers at **Mediterranee** (Haarlemmerdijk 182) make delicious pastries and sweet-dough piz-zas. But what they're really famous for is their **vegan croissants**, which are also available in whol wheat. Buy four and get the fifth one free.

I'm not crazy about the other baked goods on offer at **De Bakkerswinkel** (Warmoesstraat 69), bu the **scones** rock! Get there early, they don't last long. (It's also a pleasant and popular place fc soup and a sandwich.)

Melly's Cookie Bar (Nieuwezijds Voorburgwal 137) is a sweet little take-out cookie café just stone's throw from Dam Square. Stop by when you've got a hankering for some home-style bak ing. They serve excellent espresso here, too. A couple of doors down is a fantastic **juice bar** calle **Fruteria** owned by the same folks—a local favorite. Juicing is popular in Amsterdam, fresh fru juices, smoothies and various vegetable blends can be found citywide.

Lovers of **Italian ice cream** should head straight for **Gelateria Peppino** (Eerste Sweelinckstraa 16) near the Albert Cuyp market. They've been making it fresh daily, on the premises, for decades It's the real thing. **Ijscuypje** is a chain of ice cream shops offering freshly made flavors (cinnamor gingerbread cookie and coconut to name a few) and daily specials. Find them in the Centruum a Prinsengracht 292 and Haarlemerdijk 14.

Tiramisu fans prepare for oral exstasy at **Pane e Olio** (Oude Leliestraat 6) where premium dar chocolate is grated on their secret-recipe, famous Italian dessert.

Febo is a chain of automats all over the city. Here you can get greasy **deep-fried snacks** out of wall for about one euro. If you have to do it, your best bet is probably the kaas (cheese) soufflé. I you're feeling bold, and carnivorous, go local—eat a kroket. Basically, meat-laced deep-fried grav topped with yellow mustard. Here are a few locations: Damrak 6 (just down from Centraal Station Kalverstraat 142; Nieuwendijk 220. They're open every night 'til 3:00.

Pizza slices in Amsterdam are everywhere, but most of them are pretty terrible. Luckily, a fev places in the center have killer fare. Check out **Talia** (Prinsenstraat 12) where the tasty Roman style organic square bread pizza is a house favorite. They also offer Italian Panini, eggplant parmesanc panna cotta and varying pasta dishes. You can catch musical and culinary happenings here, a well. More info at: www.i-talia.net. **New York Pizza** (Leidsestraat 23; Spui 2; Damstraat 24) use to have the best American-style slices in town, but their quality has been declining for the pas few years. **Da Portare Via** (Leliegracht 34) sells only whole pizzas, but they are prepared usin the freshest ingredients then cooked the Italian way in a wood-burning oven. They're available i the evening from 17-22:00 and a small cheese is perfect for one person. Treat yourself to a glas of wine or an authentic espresso while you wait and watch the fire work it's magic. In the last fev years more wood oven pizzerias have opened. Check out **La Perla** (Tweede Tuindwarstraat 14, i the Jordaan neighborhood) or **De Pizza Bakers** (Haarlemerdijk 128, Plantage Kerklaan 2.)

night shops

Night Shops (avondwinkels) are the only places to buy groceries after the supermarkets close and they're accordingly expensive. Fruit and veggies at these shops are exorbitantly priced, but all the usual junk foods are available. Most night shops are open every day from 16 to 1:00. After that, you're fucked. Here are a few in the Centrum:

Pinguin Nightshop - Berenstraat 5, between the Prinsengracht and the Keizersgracht. (Map area C5)

Big Bananas - Leidsestraat 73

This night shop is usually busy because of its central location. (Map area C6)

Avondmarkt - de Wittenkade 94

This one is the biggest and most fully stocked in town with the best selection and prices, but it's in the West End. They have a full take-out counter with lasagna, pasta dishes and Indonesian food plus bonuses like organic bread and a good import beer selection. (Map area B2)

Sterk - Waterlooplein 241

Beer, wine, champagne, cigarettes and deli items are available here: cold cuts, salads and cheeses too. (Map area E6)

Baltus T - Vijzelstraat 127. (Map area D7)

Dolf - Willemsstraat 79 - In the Jordaan. (Map area C2)

Texaco - Sarphatistraat 225; Marnixstraat 250

Open 24 hours. Eat here and get gas. (Map areas H6, B5)

late night eating

De Prins - Weteringschans 1

Right across the street from the Paradiso (see Music chapter) for your after-concert french-fry craving. Open: Sun-Thurs 'til 3; Fri-Sat 'til 4. (Map area C7)

Ben Cohen - Rozengracht 239

Eating snack-bar shoarma can be a mystery-meat experience, and it's probably best to avoid the majority of them. This late-night shoarma joint, however, is one of the best in Amsterdam and a well-known local after-hours stop. For €6 you get a pita stuffed fat. Vegetarians can go for the *pita kaas*, a gooey grilled-cheese sandwich in pita bread with lettuce and cucumber. Open: Weekdays 'til 3, Weekends 'til 4

Bojo - Lange Leidsedwarsstraat 51

This Indonesian restaurant near the Leidseplein is a good place for a late-night pig-out (see Restaurants, below). Open: Sun-Thurs 'til 2; Fri-Sat 'til 4. (Map area C7)

Favorite Chicken & Ribs - Oudezijds Voorburgwal 64

Favorite is a U.K. style, late-night fried chicken joint in the Red Light district. Not the best you've eaten but more than agreeable at two in the morning. (Map area E4) food

Snackbar de Dijk - Haarlemmerdijk 145

Here's another snack shop to satisfy late-night munchies. They have french fries (€1.25), sandwiches (from €1.50), kebabs (€3.75), and lots of junk food. Open: Sun-Thurs 'til 2; Fri-Sat 'til 3. (Map area C2)

Febo Snackbars - Oudezijds Voorburgwal 33

If you're craving greasy snacks in the Red Light District Febo is open late and they're cheap (see Street Food, above). Do what you gotta do. Open: Sun-Thurs 'til 3; Fri-Sat 'til 4.

New York Pizza - Leidsestraat 23, Damstraat 24

Pizza slices until late…but not great. (see Street Food, above). Open: Sun-Thurs 'til 3; Fri-Sat 'til 4 (Map area C6, D5)

Bakkerij de Rond - Overtoom 496

This bakery has been (illegally) selling their products before opening hours for over 30 years! The city council is debating whether to stop de Rond from selling fresh baked goods to creatures of the night If you're out in the West on a Saturday morning anytime after 4:30, stick it to the man by buying some bread. It's not too far from OT301 (see Music chapter).

bread

Le Marche - Kalverstraat 201; Rokin 160

Despite the crowds, which can be daunting, Le Marche offers delicious fresh breads like multi-grain multi-seed, or garlic/thyme. They also bake panini, focaccia, pizzas and sell ready-made sandwiches plus fresh juices and yoghurt smoothies. Open: Mon-Sat 10-19 (Thurs 'til 21); Sun 12-18. (Map area D6)

Bakery Paul Annee - Runstraat 25, ☎ 623-5322; Bellamystraat 2, ☎ 618-3113

www.paulannee.n

Exclusively organic items are sold at this famous bakery. Their dark chocolate muffins are seriously addictive. They also sell sandwiches and delicious curry seitan rolls. Open: Mon-Fri 8-18; Sat 8:30-1 (Map area C5)

Gebr. Niemeijer - Nieuwendijk 35, ☎ 707-6752

www.gebroedersniemeijer.n

This French-style bakery has authentic croissants and incredible bread (the fig walnut is fantastic). They also have scrumptious pastries, sandwiches and coffees. Prices here seem a bit steep, but the fresh mostly organic ingredients and artisan baking will make you moan with pleasure after each bite. Open Tues-Fri 8-18:30, Sat. 8:30-5 (Map area: D3)

Uprising - Groen van Prinstererstraat 102, ☎ 686-0333

Part of the "handmade bread alliance" this tiny west end bakery bakes fresh organic bread, curran buns, and various scrumptious treats 6 days a week, from morning till evening. The owner, Gerhard, is also a herbalogist and sells coca leaf tea, among other potions and elixirs. Westerpark is culturally ar upcoming neighborhood, the sleepy streets now seeing funky bakeries, hip bars (the Jet Lounge, see Bars), and all sorts of cool little shops and restaurants. Open: Mon-Sat 8-18 (Map area: A2)

free samples

I don't know how desperate you are but...

Stalls at the Organic Farmers' Markets (see Shopping chapter) are a great source of free samples. Natuurwinkel supermarkets have free coffee and espresso. The bigger Albert Heijn branches offer cheese samples. Bertolli Toscaanse Lunchroom (Leidsestraat 54) has baskets of bread and a variety of olive oils to sample. And finally, it's not food but the Body Shop (Kalverstraat 157) displays tester bottles of all their lotions, creams and perfumes. Just because you're travelling doesn't mean you can't smell good.

breakfast

I love breakfast. Sometimes I can eat it three meals a day. Most hotels offer some kind of breakfast, usually bread and spread. If yours doesn't, or you find it not up to scratch, check out one of these places. An *uitsmijter* (pronounced "outsmyter") – literally, a bouncer – is a typical Dutch dish served to late-night guests just before you bounce them from your flat. It usually comprises three fried eggs with cheese, ham or roast beef served on white toast--not something special, but filling and usually pretty cheap.

Café Vennington - Prinsenstraat 2, ☎ 625-9398

Nestled in a *Jordaan* side street, Vennington is a breakfast and lunch joint with a large menu and reasonable prices. The sandwiches range in price from €2.50 for a simple Dutch cheese on a hard roll to €7.50 for a double BLT club. Their mango ice-cream shake is a sweet treat. They have a small terrace out front and if you're lucky, you can grab a table in the sun...while there's sun, of course. Never a guarantee in Amsterdam! Open: Daily 8-17. (Map area C3)

Café Latei - Zeedijk 143, ☎ 625-7485

Latei, one of Amsterdam's coolest cafés (see Cafés chapter), has a breakfast special for €7 that includes coffee or tea, orange juice, a croissant and a cheese sandwich. They also make *uitsmijters* and omelettes starting at €4, which means you can have one with a coffee and get out for about €6. It's right by the Nieuwmarkt. Open: Mon-Wed 8-18; Tues-Fri 8-22; Sat 9-22; Sun 11-18. (Map area E4)

Café Latei

food

Letting - Prinsenstraat 3, ☎ 627-9393

www.letting.nl

Letting is located on a charming little street between two canals. It's a comfortable place to drink a pot of tea and read the paper while you wait for your breakfast. Egg dishes include a mushroom omelette with a salad and toast, or an *uitsmijter* made with 3 eggs. Yoghurt with muesli and fruit, juice, and coffee or tea is €8.50. They also serve a variety of grilled tosties on Turkish bread. B-fast is served all day, and if the weather is good they have tables out front. If it's too crowded, try Vennington (Prinsenstraat 2; 625-9398), the little yellow place across the street. Kitchen open: Daily from 8-17. (Map area C3)

Drie Graefjes - Eggertstraat 1, Rokin 128 ☎ 626-6787

Mind-blowing carrot cake complete with real cream-cheese icing (€3.50) is my personal pick here, but this beautiful little café nestled in a small, historic alley off Dam Square has much more. Besides amazing homemade desserts, muffins and cookies, Drie Graefjes offers a complete breakfast and lunch menu. Scrambled eggs with onion, tomatoes and fresh bread costs €5.50 (add €1.50 for smoked salmon). A fresh bowl of soup is €4.75 and the sandwiches, from simple Dutch cheese to a stacked club, run from €4-€7.50. Sit on the terrace if there's room and the weather cooperates. A new Drie Graefjes sits on the busy Rokin.
Open: Daily 9-18 (Map area D4)

Lef - Wijde Heisteeg 1, ☎ 620-5768

Lef means courage in Dutch. I don't know why you'd need it here though, because this little café is about as non-threatening as they come. It's petite, colorful, has a cozy upstairs and the smallest terrace in Amsterdam—a fold-down bench out front with a couple of pillows on it. They have egg breakfasts for around €7, fresh juices, smoothies and sandwiches on all sorts of bread. Don't miss their fresh-baked brownies.
Open: Mon-Fri 9:30-16; Sat-Sun 11-17. (Map area C6)

Barney's Uptown - Haarlemmerstraat 105, ☎ 427-9469

www.barneys.biz

Feel like a joint and a stack of pancakes? Barney's Uptown is the premier spot for waking and baking. You can get breakfast here all day and they also have a full lunch and dinner menu. At night it's a cool bar where DJs regularly spin (see Bars). Located just across the street from Barney's Coffeeshop. Open: Mon-Thurs 8-1; Fri-Sat 7:30-3, Sun 7:30-1. (Map area D3)

Bazar - Albert Cuypstraat 182, ☎ 675-0544

Check out this huge Turkish breakfast: pita and simit breads, marinated feta cheese, cream cheese with herbs, apricot jam, honey, a Turkish pancake, yoghurt with fresh fruit, a boiled egg, sausage, juice and coffee or tea—all that for €7.90, or €15.25 for two. You can also have a lighter meal of mild yoghurt, fruit salad, and fresh OJ for €5.25, or an omelette with pita and salad for €4.90. By the time you're finished, the market outside will be in full swing. Check the restaurant section below for a full description of this funky place. Open from 8 Mon-Fri; and 9 Sat-Sun.

Lunchcafé Nielsen - Berenstraat 19, ☎ 330-6006

They serve a full breakfast here (see Restaurants, below) for around €10, or if you want *à la carte* they've got yoghurt, fruit salads, croissants, and organic bacon. Open: Tues-Fri 8-16; Sat 8-18; Sun 9-17 (Map Area C5)

Winkel Lunchcafé - Noordermarkt 43, ☎ 623 -0223

If you're visiting one of the markets by the Noorderkerk on Saturday or Monday morning (see Markets

Shopping chapter), make a stop at this famous café on the square's corner. They serve the best apple pie in Amsterdam. Everyone gets a piece and sits outside drinking cappuccino or fresh mint tea at shared tables. They've recently extended their hours to stay open late as well as early. Open: Mon 7-1; Tues-Thurs 8-1; Fri 8-2; Sat 7-2; Sun 10-24. (Map area C3)

Rembrandt's Birthday Breakfast - Rijksmuseum

To celebrate Rembrandt's birthday on July 15 the Rijksmuseum (see Museum chapter) serves a free breakfast in its garden every year. It's not a big spread, just coffee and some bread and herring, but the price is right! Last year the museum was free on that day, too. Be there by 7:30 if you want to get some chow. (Map area C8)

Wintergarden (Hotel Krasnapolsky) - Dam 9, ☎ 554-9111

For a splurge, treat yourself to Hotel Krasnapolsky's breakfast buffet at their 19th-century Wintergarden, where you can eat your fill for €27.50. From the tiled floor to the abundant plants and grand murals to the wrought-iron balustrade and the glass roof almost 14 meters above you, it's spectacular. Open: Daily 6:30-10:30. (Map area D4)

restaurants

Affordable gourmet food is rare here, but there are eateries serving high quality, flavorful food at decent prices. Avoid the dozens of tourist-strip restaurants with guys standing out front trying to con you in – they always suck! Most of the places I recommend are friendly to tourists (as they should be), but remember that Amsterdam is not always known for hospitable service. Here, as in most European cities, you need to signal the server if you want something. Also, make sure you've got enough cash on you because many of the following places don't take credit cards. Okay, now go eat.

Mok Sam - Albert Cuyp 65, ☎ 679-6776

Surinamese/Chinese. This plain little joint is next door to another restaurant with basically the same menu; I stumbled in here first, so this is the one I frequent. They have cheap noodle dishes, rotis and a large selection of soups and sandwiches. For dessert try *bakabana* – deep-fried battered banana strips with spicy/sweet peanut sauce for €1. Now that's what I'm talkin' about! Located near the Albert Cuyp market (see Markets, Shopping chapter). Open: Daily 11-22.

Eat at Jo's - Marnixstraat 409, ☎ 638-3336

Everything. This restaurant is run by a couple who go that extra mile (they're from America or I would have said kilometer) to make sure the food is tasty and the service is good. Full-course, lovingly prepared meals cost about €11 for a vegetarian set menu and about €14 for meat or fish. The servings are huge and there's plenty of variety: The menu changes regularly and on any given night you might be choosing between a meal that's Italian-themed, Japanese-inspired, or North African-flavored. The homemade desserts are amazing; I had a whopping piece of chocolate cake that was so good I almost cried. Eat at Jo's is located in the Melkweg (see Music chapter) and often the band playing there that evening will be dining at the table next to you. Whether the place is half-empty and mellow or full and hectic, whether you want a full meal or just a snack and a beer, it's always relaxed and comfortable here. You can also order a drink and take it with you into the photo gallery in the next room. Open: Wed-Sun 12-21. (Map area C7)

Burgermeester - Albert Cuypstraat 48, ☎ 670-9339, Plantage Kerklaan 37, Elandsgracht 130

www.burgermeester.eu

Burgers. This gourmet burger joint uses primarily Netherlands produce. Burgermeester's honest food policy means that all the ingredients are either organic or locally raised, a responsible practice more restaurants should follow. They have eight different burgers (beef, lamb or veggie) ranging from €6 to €8 (or mini versions for half price) and a burger-of-the-month from patron-submitted recipes. A portion of the proceeds from burger-of-the-month sales goes to a charity of the winner's choice. Divine desserts, like lemon cheesecake with raspberry sauce (€3), are made fresh daily, and they have a luscious juice bar. Everything here – from juice combinations to which ingredients you want on your burger – can be custom-ordered. WiFi connected. Open: Daily 12-23.

Burrito - De Clerqstraat 14, ☎ 618-9807

Mexican. Fans of good Mexican food, a rarity in Europe, will like Burrito, a little family-run restaurant with renowned chimichangas, delicious stewed meat tacos, big combination plates (taco/enchilada €13.50), quesadillas and, of course, fat burritos. They put salad with 1000 Island dressing on all their plates unless you ask otherwise and if you order spicy, they stuff pickled jalapeños in their food, which I personally don't dig – try their homemade hot sauce instead. Margaritas and Mexican beer cool the fire. Open: Tues-Sun 4-10:30 (Map area A5)

Soprano - Vijzelstraat 97, ☎ 427-7881

Italian. This is where Italian Amsterdammers go for authentic midday meals. And now this popular little restaurant is open for dinner, too. Soprano offers dishes like homemade pasta with mushroom cream sauce or crunchy-crusted ciabatta with Italian meatballs. All pasta dishes are €9, and though the plates aren't huge, the quality is superb. Add a piece of decadent chocolate cake for dessert plus a drink and you're enjoying top-rate Italian for around €15. *Buon appetito!* Open: Tue-Sat 12-15, 17-22. (Map area D7)

The Taco Shop - Tolstraat 200, ☎ 470-3657

Mexican. The Taco Shop, from its Miami-green paint job to the Memphis blues on the stereo, is a little piece of the U.S. along Amsterdam's Amstel river offering American-style Mexican fast food. A huge refried bean tostada (€5.50) topped with lettuce, cheese, tomatoes and sour cream is a meal in itself. They also have hard-shell tacos, burritos, chimichangas and quesadillas, and will gladly customize orders to your dietary desires. All the orders include tortilla chips on the side. Expats are known to frequent this shop, as well as famous Yankee musicians whose autographs adorn the walls – from Lou Reed to System of a Down. It's a bit far out of the center, but if you're jonesing for a burrito it's worth the trek. Open: Daily 12-22.

Vliegende Schotel (Flying Saucer) - Nieuwe Leliestraat 162, ☎ 625-2841

www.vliegendeschotel.com

Vegetarian. This restaurant is situated in the beautiful *Jordaan* (pronounced "Yordahn") neighborhood, so make sure to take a walk before or after your meal. They have a big menu, mostly organic, that includes some vegan dishes and half-servings are also available. Lots of locals eat here. Open: Daily 16-23:30 (but the last call for dinner orders is at 22:45). (Map area B4)

My Burrito - Kinkerstraat 142, ☎ 412-5526

www.myburrito.nl

Mexican. Fat burritos made to order are the specialties at this west side eatery—I'm fiending for one now as I write this sentence. The owner's enthusiasm for San Francisco-style rice and bean burritos led him to perfect his wrapping craft and open a little Amsterdam based open-kitchen restaurant. He offers veggie or organic ground beef, black bean or pinto bean and rice burritos for around €6, with homemade salsa as hot and thick as you want it. If you go for the works (guacamole, sour cream and lettuce) then it's a tad extra. The menu is kept simple: daily specials, burritos, tacos and quesadillas, but they're done right and made with high quality organic ingredients. Eat here immediately if you're a burrito freak like me. Open: Tue- Sat 14-20, Sun- Mon 14-20. (Map area A6)

Pondok Indah - Prinsengracht 42, ☎ 422-0029

Indonesian. An Indonesian couple runs this little hole-in-the-wall where a delicious variety of meat and vegetarian dishes are prepared and displayed in a glass case. The best deal is the "Box2Go," a small box with either noodles or fried rice and your choice of any two dishes for only €4.95. If you're really hungry or are sharing, you can get a bigger box for €6.95. There are all kinds of other Indonesian specialties too, and they speak English, so you won't have any problem finding out what's what. There are a couple of stools inside, but this is really a take-out place. Grab your food and walk north (toward Centraal Station) for a few minutes and—for genuine canal-side dining Amsterdam style–just past the Noorderkerk, you'll find a couple of benches across the bridge. (Map area C3)

Restaurant Welcome - Zeedijk 57, ☎ 638-6234

Vietnamese. Asian cuisine abounds in Amsterdam—Chinese, Indonesian, Thai, Japanese—but quality Vietnamese food is a rarity. Welcome is truly the star of southeast Asian cooking, from the huge bowls of famous hot and sour *Pho* (rice noodle soup, €11) to the scrumptious *Goi Cuon* (shrimp and mint leaf rice paper rolls, €4.50). Their seafood fried rice (€11.50) includes fresh shrimp, scallops and cuttlefish—add a dash of Vietnamese hot sauce for a sublime taste experience. Vegetarians have a variety of options here as well. The menu has some seriously pricey items, like lobster or a seafood fondue banquet, but you also find great food for a decent price even travel writers can afford. So good, I actually want to keep it a secret. Open: Daily 12-23. (Map area E4)

Kagetsu - Van Woustraat 29, Hartenstraat 17; ☎ 662-7340

Japanese. You'll find this unassuming yet stylish Japanese joint in De Pijp near the famous Albert Cuyp Market. The décor is simple and the comic-style hand-drawn menus add a humorous touch. The sushi rocks and the young chef adds his own flare to the rolls, like spicy tuna with purple onion and homemade hot sauce. A salmon-and-avocado hand roll costs €4.50; nigiri sushi runs from €3.50-€4.50 per two pieces. Warm dishes run from €7.50 (vegetables and fried Soba noodles) to €15 (steak with sweet soy sauce). There's a traditional Japanese-style room in the back where larger groups can eat. Kagetsu is unique for its decent prices and high-quality authentic eats, as evidenced by a steady Japanese clientele. Feel like seriously splurging? Try the Master's Choice, where the chef makes a combination meal customized to your culinary desires. There's another teeny tiny Kagetsu at Hartenstraat 17 (Map area C5) in Amsterdam's charming *Neger Straatjes* (Nine Streets) area and a grill and noodle-specialized Kagestu (Kastelenstraat 268) further out of the Centrum. Open: Tues-Sun 17-23. Kastelenstraat: 18-00.

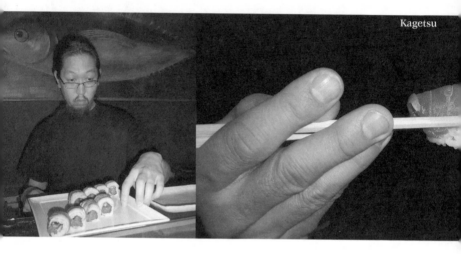

Kagetsu

SushiMe - Oude Leliestraat 7, 627-7926; Delivery: ☎ 627-7043

www.sushime.nl

Japanese. This stark sushi outlet just off the Herengracht sits right across the street from Foodism (see Restaurants chapter) and the Grey Area (see Coffeeshops). The décor is stern but I found the sushi to be just about the best in town, with combi menus starting at €6.90 and the Big Maki Menus from €13.50. They offer soups, salads, sashimi, delicious handrolls, a veggie menu, and there's fresh ginger for your sushi. "Some Rules to Remember" from some other time and place are stenciled on the wall but they're probably best ignored. Credit cards, however, are welcomed. Open: Daily 14-22. (Map area C4)

Chao Phraya - Nieuwmarkt 8-10, ☎ 427-6334

Thai. On a sunny day Chao Phraya is a great place to get your phad thai and clock the interesting human activity in the Nieuwmarkt from your sidewalk table outside the restaurant. It's nice inside too, and the staff is exceptionally warm and friendly. It's not cheap, but the rice or noodle dishes with beef, chicken or shrimp from €13-€15.00 are well prepared and deliver everything you could ask for in a Thai meal. Credit cards cheerfully accepted. Open: Daily 12-22. (Map area: E5)

O'cha - Binnenbantammerstraat 1, ☎ 625-9958

Thai. If you like curries that hurt so good, you'll appreciate this homey restaurant run by two Thai sisters. A huge bowl of green curry costs €9 (tofu) to €13 (prawn) and can easily be shared. Last time I ate here, I was sweating like I had just run a marathon but still sporting a scarlet-faced smile. One of the sisters kept handing me napkins to wipe the perspiration from my brow. Less masochistic curry fans can ask for mild. Open: Daily 15-23. (Map area E4)

New King - Zeedijk 115-117, ☎ 625-2810

Chinese. New King, one of Amsterdam's most popular Chinese restaurants, is an authentic, affordable dining experience. Just thinking about their crispy fried noodles (€9) makes me salivate, and their salt-and-pepper shrimp is insanely good. They have a massive menu, prompt service and—as a real bonus—free jasmine tea with your meal. Located in the heart of Chinatown. (Map area E4)

Thais Snackbar Bird - Zeedijk 77, ☎ 420-6289
www.thai bird.nl

Thai. If you've ever been to Thailand you'll appreciate this tiny place. It's got the atmosphere down pat, with Thai pop songs, pictures of the king, and orchids on the tables. The meals aren't super cheap but the food is always prepared fresh and it's delicious (like heavenly Tom Ka Kai soup) – well worth the walk through the sleazy Amsterdam version of Chinatown. Open: Daily 15-22. (Map area E4)

Kam Yin - Warmoesstraat 6, ☎ 625-3115

Surinamese/Chinese. Kam Yin is one of the cheapest noodle and rice restaurants in Amsterdam, and it's extremely centrally located—two minutes from Centraal Station. They have a big take-away menu (including roti, fat sandwiches and spring rolls) and the servings are huge. Dishes start as low as €4.50 and one main dish along with a side order is probably enough for two people. You can also eat in for just a little bit more. Open: Daily 12-24. (Map area E4)

Planet Rose - Nicolaas Beetsstraat 47, ☎ 612-9838

Jamaican. Luscious fresh dishes prepared with love make this little out-of-the-way restaurant a must for Jamaican/Caribbean food lovers and anyone who appreciates home-style cooking. Rose, the owner and chef, is a gracious host and her meals—from a scrumptious vegetarian curry to jerk chicken or salmon—are a good deal. Small plates are €9 and large plates €15. A piece of freshly made cake, like the delicious coconut cake with custard I devoured, costs €6. The menu changes daily and all the meals include salad, rice and peas plus fried plantains. You need a bit of patience—the food is all freshly made—but your belly will be rewarded. Located out of the center in the West near the Ten Kate Markt (see Shopping/Markets). Take tram 17 (direction Osdorp) and get off at Ten Kate Markt, walk down the market street, take the first left, walk a small block and it's on the corner. It's a bit of a mission to get here but you won't regret it. Cash Only. Open: Tues-Sat 14-22; Sun 17-22

Restaurant Yummie - Haarlemmerdijk 6, ☎ 330-3985
www.yummie-sushi.nl

Japanese. This simple looking Japanese joint brings masterful technique to the masses: inexpensive but high quality sushi in a casual settting. Yummie has one of Amsterdam's best sushi and teppanyaki chefs who was wrangled away from a famous high-end restaurant. Spicy salmon handrolls (€3.50), scallop sashimi (4 pieces, €4) and shrimp tempura (€5,50) are just a few examples of the excellently priced fare. Add a cold Japanese beer and full culinary contentment is yours. Just a ten-minute stroll from Centraal Station. Open every day, 16-22. (Map area: C2)

Moti Mahal - Nieuwezijds Voorburgwal 34, ☎ 625-0330
www.motimahal.nl

Indian. This traditional Indian restaurant in the Kolk serves some of the finest tandoori and other Indian specialties in a warm, relaxing atmosphere with excellent service and a top-notch chef. Everything on the menu is tasty and their lamb is particularly succulent and never tough or stringy. Their vindaloos will warm you down to the cockles of your heart. Open: Daily 17-22 (Map area D4)

Lunchcafé Nielsen - Berenstraat 19, ☎ 330-6006

Healthy Diner. Before or after you finish exploring the little streets in the charming *Negen Straatje* (Nine Streets) area, stop by this family-run café for a freshly prepared breakfast or lunch. But don't b in a rush: the tasty food draws a crowd, and it's always busy. Nielsen has an English menu with plent of vegetarian choices, a few vegan options, and only free-range meat. A full breakfast costs aroun €10, or you can get items like fruit salad or an omelet, à la carte. They also have sandwiches from €4.7 to €9.50, giant salads from €9.25, and homemade soups from €5. *Eet smakelijk.* Open: Tues-Fri 8-16 Sat 8-18; Sun 9-17. (Map Area C5)

Maoz Vegetarian - Damrak 40, ☎ 625-0717

Falafel. Over the years this falafel take-away has grown in reputation and store numbers. The newes branch is just a skip from Centraal Station. A whole-wheat pita stuffed with 5 falafel balls, fried eggplan and limitless salad bar is only €4.30 for a small and €5 for a large. This particular Maoz includes cauliflow er pakorma (yum!) in the salad offerings. For veggie fast food this is the place. Note: the green sauce i smoking hot; usually they warn you, but not always. Other outlets include: Muntplein1, Leidsestraat 8! and the original Maoz at Reguliersbreestraat 45, near Rembrandtplein. Open: Daily 11-1. (Map area D4)

Foodism - Oude Leliestraat 8, ☎ 427-5103

Everything. This funky little restaurant is on the same pretty street as Grey Area (see Coffeeshops, Cannabis chapter) and has a sign on the door that says "Sorry, We're Open." They make homemade soups, salads, filling sandwiches and delicious vegetarian ravioli. It's a place you can walk into wrecked after an all-night bender and feel comfortable listening to some chilled tunes, enjoying a big plate o scrambled eggs, salmon and a bagel. Open Mon-Sat "around 10:30 til 22," Sun 12-18. (Map area C4)

Morning Star - Nieuwezijds Voorburwal (opposite 289), ☎ 620-3302

Everything. This place used to be called Dolores and was known for organic burgers, good coffee and super-friendly service. Luckily, the new owners adhere to the same standards: fresh food, lots of healthy options and a pleasant terrace. One great Amsterdam food trend is the addition of organic and healthy items to menus; Morning Star sticks to this recipe and offers an organic beef burger with fries for €8.50. You can get the veggie equivalent for €6.00. Or why not go exotic—an organic chicken focaccia sandwich with spicy sweet peanut sauce (€5.50). Other menu items include soups, salads and scrumptious desserts. The kitchen is in a beautiful little historic cottage. There are only a couple of stools along the bar inside, but the picnic-table terrace is roomy. Grab a fruit shake (€3.50) or a soy latte and enjoy a bit of modern Amsterdam café life. Located near Dam Square. Open: Mon-Fri 6-16. (Map area C5)

De Peper - Overtoom 301

www.ot301.nl

Organic Vegan. This former film school was squatted after sitting empty for some time and now houses several studios and workshops, a radio station, a movie theatre (see Film chapter), living spaces, and a great restaurant called De Peper. It's very popular so make sure you call at 16:00 to reserve a meal. Let them know when you arrive, and then kick back with a beer or juice. Everything on offer is organic – even the cognac. The bar opens at 18:00 and the food is served at about 19:00. The meal consists of soup and a carefully prepared main course. De Peper is renowned for cheap, healthy, vegan food, including tasty desserts. At the moment they're cooking full meals on Tuesday, Thursday, Friday and Sunday nights. There are often DJs and performances after dinner and the bar stays open until 1:00 (3:00 on Fridays), so you can also arrive later for drinks. From Leidseplein it's about a 10-minute walk, or you can hop on tram 1. (Map area A7)

Burger Bar - Kolksteeg 2, ☎ 624-9049

Burgers. Burger Bar is one of the first and definitely one of the best places to enjoy Amsterdam's new-ish food trend. Choose your roll, the burger size and the sauces you want, and a cooked-to-order burger will run you between €4.95 and €12.95 (the Kobe Beef version.) Fresh-cut French fries with a choice of 21 sauces are also on the menu. Take a seat in the charming 17th-century alleyway outside and they'll bring your grub to you. Located off the Nieuwendijk, 5 minutes walk from Central Station. Another larger Burger Bar, replete with diner style décor, is near Rembrandtplein at Reguliersbreestraat 9 (map area D6) and the newest branch is centrally located at Warmoestraat 21 (map area D4). Open: Sun-Thurs 11-3; Fri-Sat 'till 4. (Map area D4)

Kismet - Albert Cuypstraat 64, ☎ 671-4768

Turkish. If you've never tried Turkish food, Kismet is an ideal place to start. Much of what's on offer is tantalizingly displayed in the window, but they also have other dishes like lentil soup and calorie-packed moussaka. Most items cost only a few euros, so it's easy to try several things amongst a group of friends. Or you can order one of their set menus that start at €9.50 for a big plate of stuffed eggplant, assorted veggies, filled grape leaves, rice and potatoes. For the same price, meat eaters can get the eggplant and veggies with chicken and a meatball. You'll be stuffed, but try to save room for some of their delicious baklava with your coffee. When the weather's warm they have tables outside. Avoid the peak meal hours if you can, because this is a small place and they're often full. Another even smaller Kismet specializing in freshly baked, unbelievably tasty Turkish pizza is at Kinkerstraat 350, five minutes walk from the Ten Katemarkt (see Shopping). The Albert Cuypstraat location is a stone's throw from the Albert Cuyp market. Open: Daily 8-20.

Addis Ababa - Overtoom 337, ☎ 618-4472

www.addisababa.nl

Ethiopian. Addis Ababa is a great restaurant to go with a bunch of friends. Spicy edibles are served on giant Ethiopian-style pancake-laden platters in the traditional way, and everybody eats with their hands, wrapping the tasty food morsels in the njere bread. The decor is lively and the owner's hospitality renowned. They serve several veggie dishes and something for carnivores too. Try a Banana Beer with your meal to help alleviate the spice. Open: Daily 17-23. (Map area A7)

Olive & Cookie - Saenredamstraat 67, ☎ 470-7190

Gourmet Food. Considering their minute workspace, the variety and array of delicious food produced at Olive & Cookie is astonishing. Edibles here all taste as good as they look. The friendly owners sell everything you need for a complete gourmet meal: vegetarian tapas, salads, savory pies, casseroles, fresh soups and incredible desserts. It's all organic and sold by weight or by the piece. The menu changes regularly, always including vegan options, and you never know what oven-fresh delights await your salivating mouth. Most of it is take-out, but there are also a few seats and a table if you just can't wait. There's no meat, but they do cook fish. Olive & Cookie is located on a small side street in De Pijp. Open: Mon-Sat 13-21.

Soup En Zo - Jodenbreestraat 94a, ☎ 422-2243

www.soupenzo.nl

Soup. A popular addition to Amsterdam's culinary scene is the soup stall, especially on cold, wet days (lotsa those in this city). The cooks in this little restaurant use fresh, often organically-grown vegetables in their soups, and there are always several vegetarian options. They also serve salads and Brazilian fruit shakes. In nice weather there are tables out front. Soup en Zo is located close to the Waterlooplein market. There is another shop at Nieuwe Spiegelstraat 54, but it's for take-away only. Jodenbreestraat location open: Mon-Fri 11-20; Sat-Sun 12-19. (Map area E6)

Soepwinkel - Eerste Sweelinckstraat 19, ☎ 673-2293

www.soepwinkel.nl

Soup. The "Soup Store" terrace, spacious by Amsterdam standards, sits on a side street between the Albert Cuyp market and Sarphatipark. It's a great spot to kick back and relax while you sample the tasty goods like Caribbean sweet potato and Tunisian vegetable soups. Regularly changing menus include mostly seasonal and locally grown vegetables. Prices start at €3.95 for a small bowl and bread, and go up to €10.50 for a large, which is huge! There's a set menu for €7.90 that includes a bowl of soup, a small piece of quiche and a drink. Peppino's (see Street Food, above) is just across the street and their ice cream is an ideal way to finish off a meal. Soepwinkel open: Mon-Fri 11-20; Sat 11-18.

La Place Grand Café Restaurant - Kalverstraat 201, ☎ 622-0171

www.laplace.nl

Everything. Occupying a couple of little 17th-century houses, this department-store food court lacks the usual fast-food crap and atmosphere. Most of what's offered in the main floor *menagerie* –stir-fries, steaks, fish, pasta and salads – is prepared in little open kitchens and then invitingly displayed for you to help yourself (€1.25 for 100 grams). Fill up a container and your meal is weighed to calculate the price. They also have sandwiches on panini for €3, pizza for €3.35 a slice, plus brownies, cookies and a variety of desserts. Upstairs you'll find elegant little booths that display a wide variety of fruits and vegetables bought directly from the producers. The menu changes daily and everything is prepared fresh. Here are some of the cheaper examples from the last time I was here: Soup of the day, €3.50; French fries, €1.95; hot chocolate with whipped cream, €1.90. There are also a couple of salad bars – fruit (€3) and vegetable (€3.30) – where you can test your architectural skills by piling a plate as high as possible. Full meals cost between €6-€12. Up another flight there's a small balcony over the Kalverstraat that's great for people watching, if the weather is nice. Open: Sun-Mon 11-20; Tues-Sat 10-20; (Thurs 'til 21). (Map area D6)

Einde van de Wereld (End of the World) - Javakade (opposite number 21), KNSM Island

Home Cooking. Some years back, with a lot of hard work by volunteers, the lively atmosphere of this famous squat restaurant was transplanted onto a boat. Step down into the hold of the ship and there's a bright, bustling room filled with great music and the smell of home cooking. There's a choice of a vegetarian (€6) or an organic meat dish (€8) – half plates are also available (lots of kids here: see Kids section). Dessert costs €2. Though the deliciousness quotient varies, it's always a good deal: The servings are huge and there's also bread and garlic butter on the tables. Drinks are cheap. Order your meal at the bar, leave your name, pay, and in about 15 minutes they'll bring you your food. In good weather, take your beer and sit up top overlooking the water. The boat's name is Quo Vadis and there's little sign in front. You can take bus 42 from Centraal Station eastbound (it'll say KNSM Eiland on the front) to the Azartplein. Head towards the big bridge and then turn right and walk along the water. Or better yet, take a bicycle so you can cruise around a bit before or after your meal: The interesting architecture in this newly built neighborhood is world-renowned. Einde van de Wereld is open only on Wednesdays and Fridays from 18:00. (Map area I3)

Toscana - Haarlemmerstraat 130, ☎ 622-0353; Haarlemmerdijk 176, ☎ 624-8358

Italian. I'm always complaining to visitors about how pathetic Amsterdam pizzas are. This place isn't the best in town, but all their pizzas are "half price" and I love a bargain. The cheapest pizza is a thin but big *margherita* for €4.75, which means you can have a pizza and a beer for about €7.50. Some of the pizzas, like the *Yildrim* – blue cheese, pineapple, garlic and oregano – actually rock. If you eat this one, your tastebuds will experience happy confusion but you might not be so kissable later. "When the moon hits your eye, like a big pizza pie, that's amoré…." Open: Daily 16-23. (Map area C2)

Go Freshshop
Amstelstraat 27, ☎ 428-5264; Vijzelstraat 135, ☎ 528-9865, 2nd Hugo de Grootstraat 20

www.gofreshshop.nl

The cooks at these shops adhere to the slow-food movement so don't expect a speedy meal. But if it's healthy, hearty food you crave, you're in for a treat. Meals here are prepared in an open kitchen, and all the ingredients are super fresh: nothing is chopped, diced, or grated until you order. Pasta, meat or fish dishes cost between €9 and €13. For around €4 you can choose one of over a dozen sandwiches, both warm and cold. The goat-cheese mousse with grilled eggplant and rocket salad is fantastic as is the teriyaki filet mignon with sprouts and cucumber. They're also known for their fresh juices, like the house blend – orange, apple, carrot, cuke and tomato (small €3; large €4). The newest and nicest location is on the Amstelstraat between Rembrandtplein and the Amstel River. If it's busy, get your grub to go and head around the corner to the famous Skinny Bridge (Magere Brug) for some riverside, bench dining. Or, order in to your hotel: they deliver. Amstelstraat open: Sun-Thurs 11-22; Fri-Sat 11-24. (Map area D6)

Riaz - Bilderdijkstraat 193, ☎ 683-6453

www.riaz.nl

Surinamese/Indian/Indonesian. Riaz is popular with famous Dutch football players, TV personalities, rockstars and anybody that enters the door. It's not the decor, which is simple and clean, but the amazing food that keeps the masses coming back. I like the Pom (home-made Surinamese yam and chicken casserole, served with rice, green beans and tasty sweet/sour pickles). They offer several dishes that range in price from chicken and lamb curries at €12.50. to Surinamese and Indonesian food – rice, noodles, rotis – at €6 for vegetarian dishes and €6 to €11 with meat (no pork, however: this joint is *halal*.) Snacks and sandwiches abound and the deep-fried bananas are legendary. Have a little patience while waiting for your food—all the meals are prepared fresh. Open: Sun 14-21; Mon-Fri 11:30-21. (Map area A6)

Bojo - Lange Leidsedwarsstraat 51, ☎ 626-8990 (☎ 694-2864 for hotel delivery)

www.bojo.nl

Indonesian. This place is in all the tourist guides, but a lot of Dutch people go here too because what the food lacks in excitement is made up for by the huge servings and reasonable prices (€8.50 and up). And they're open late. Skip the appetizers: they're not very good. The entrees are okay, but if you want a real Indonesian "rice table" you have to pay at least €20 per person. If you have the dough try Cilubang (Runstraat 10; 626-9755; www.cilubang.com) where the food is fantastic. Bojo is open: Mon-Thurs 16-2; Fri 16-4; Sat 12-4; Sun 12-2. (Map area C7)

food

Pannenkoekhuis Upstairs - Grimburgwal 2, ☎ 626-5603

Pancakes. Not having a pancake in Holland would be like coming here and not seeing a windmill – it's part of the Dutch experience. This cozy joint is on the second floor of a tiny, 17th century house jus east of the Spui. Prices start at about €5.50. Toppings include everything from simple powdered suga to strawberries and whipped cream to bananas with chocolate sauce. Open: Fri 12-18:30; Sat 12-17:30 Sun 12-17; Mon 12-19. Closed Tues-Thurs and the whole month of January. (Map area D5)

MKZ - Eerste Schinkelstraat 16, ☎ 679-0712

Vegan/Vegetarian. MKZ is a Dutch abbreviation for hoof-and-mouth disease, so it's no surprise the onl things slaughtered here are vegetables. Big plates of veggie fare are dished up two to four nights week by volunteer crews. For a while, the *Koken met Tieten* night (Cooks with Tits) – where the mostl female chefs worked topless – was very popular. The restaurant is at the edge of the squatted Binner pret complex on the far side of Vondelpark. You might want to combine a meal here with a visit to th sauna (see Saunas, Hanging Out chapter), or a concert at OCCII (see Music chapter). In the summe you can eat in the courtyard, but winter can get very chilly so try to snag a seat near the heater or th open kitchen. The last time I was here, soup and a main dish were only €4.50. Drinks are super cheap too: juice and tea are 50 cents, wine or a bottle of beer only €1! Call in the afternoon to find out i they're open and make a reservation. Food is served at 19.00. At the moment they're open Tues Wec and Fri, but that can change. Closed in the summer.

Café de Molli - Van Ostadestraat 55, ☎ 676-1427

www.molli.m

Vegetarian/Vegan. This place serves up big cheap eats– full veggie or vegan meals in a very basic commu nal setting. The prices are unbeatable for healthy grub. Call the number above in the afternoon to reserv your meal. For a little more info about this squat see the Cafés chapter. Meals are served at 19:00.

The Atrium - Oudezijds Achterburgwal 237, ☎ 525-3999

Caféteria food. This is a self-service student *mensa* with cheap meals. Gourmet it ain't, but damn it' cheap. Among the many offerings at lunchtime are salads for €1.25, soup for only 70 cents, grille cheese for €1, and burgers for €2.75. At dinner you can get a full meal with a main dish of meat, fish or veggie for around €6.50 (cheaper if you've got a student card). Meals are served on weekdays from 11 to 15:00 and 17 to 19:30 (Friday until 19:00), but it's open the rest of the day for drinks and snacks Closed on weekends. There's another student *mensa*, Agora, at Roetersstraat 11, that offers the same food. Same hours as the Atrium except on Friday when it closes at 16:00. (Map area D5)

Keuken van 1870 - Spuistraat 4, ☎ 620-4018

www.keukenvan1870.n

Caféteria food. Keuken opened as a soup kitchen in 1870, and you can still get a fairly cheap basic mea here. A three-course meat and potato dinner costs about €8. And they always have stampot, a tradi tional Dutch dish that comprises mashed potatoes, vegetables, and sausage or meatballs (€7). The also have an à la carte menu with a couple of vegetarian choices, but it's more of a meat-eater kind o place. Close to Centraal Station. Open: Mon-Sat 17-22. (Map area D3)

Koffiehuis Van Den Volksbond - Kadijksplein 4, ☎ 622-1209

www.koffiehuisvandenvolksbond.n

Originally this beautiful old building close to the Maritime Museum was one of many "coffee houses" throughout the city – charitable projects designed by employers and their wives to help combat alcohol ism amongst the migrant workforce. The *Koffiehuis* served cheap meals, coffee and beer (but no hard liquor) at subsidized prices to draw the men away from the bars. In the 1980s it was saved from demoli tion by squatters. Now it houses a comfortable arty restaurant serving high-quality meals, still mostly to people from the neighborhood. Prices are no longer subsidized, but it's a pleasant place to splurge

The menu changes nightly and features starters like cream of venkel soup with smoked salmon and blue cheese (€4.75) or prawns cooked in garlic and sherry €7.25). Hearty main dishes run €11 to €15 and rich desserts around €6. There are about a half-dozen choices for each course and there's always at least one veggie option. The kitchen is open daily from 18-22; Sundays they open at 17. (Map area G5)

Koffiehuis Van Den Volksbond

Hap Hmm - 1st Helmersstraat 33; ☎ 618-1884
www.hap-hmm.nl

Dutch Food. Just like dinner in Mom's kitchen. Hap Hmm is a little eatery situated on a residential street that runs parallel to the Overtoom. They serve a lot of meat and fish dishes including veggies and potatoes (average price €6.50), and lately they've been adding different sorts of vegetarian meals to the menu as well. You can also go à la carte: they have small salads for €1.75, soup of the day is €1.50, and desserts are cheap too. It's not fancy, but you get a filling Dutch meal in a homey environment. Expect the other diners to be old folk from the neighborhood along with people carrying their copies of Get Lost! Open: Mon-Fri 16:30-20. (Map area B7)

Toos & Roos - Herengracht 309, ☎ 423-6034

Home Cooking. Cooks at this cozy café use mainly organic ingredients in their scrumptious breakfast and lunch dishes. There are several tables of various sizes, but grab a seat at the counter facing the window to enjoy the canal view. Be sure to save room for dessert as they bake wonderful brownies and cakes, including sticky toffee cake (warm date cake with caramel sauce) that's joy on a fork. Open: Mon-Fri 8:30-17:30; Sat 10-17:30; Sun 12-17:30. (Map area C5)

Bazar - Albert Cuypstraat 182, ☎ 675-0544
www.bazaramsterdam.nl

North African/Turkish/Middle Eastern. Bazar is located in a huge space with ornate decorations – mosaics and colorful lights, giant chandeliers hanging over the upstairs veranda – that help create a unique dining atmosphere. They serve breakfast (see Breakfast section, above) and lunch until 17:00. Sandwiches start at €4 (the falafel is excellent) and big salads start at €7. They also have tasty soups, Turkish pizzas and other regional snacks. In the evening there's a full dinner menu of big, filling dishes – lots of kebabs, couscous, aubergine, olives and artichokes – that average about €11. There's plenty for vegetarians, and carnivores will love the mixed grill with meat or fish. It's a fun and festive place, great if you're going with a gang. Best to reserve during peak hours. Open: Mon-Thurs 8-1; Fri 8-2; Sat 9-2; Sun 9-24.

Special Bite
www.specialbite.com

Want more restaurant suggestions? For extensive, independent Amsterdam restaurant listings in all price ranges, try Special Bite. They have an excellent website that's updated regularly and a printed guide that appears quarterly. Both are in English, easy to use, and fun to read.

Cafés

Cafés are plentiful in Amsterdam, ideal places to hang out and get a feel for the city. *Bruin Cafés*, Amsterdam's version of the pub, can be found in every neighborhood; explore the *Jordaan's* charming streets and canals for authentic, Dutch cafés in the city center. Once you've ordered, you'll be left alone to read, write postcards or vegetate. Don't be shy to share a table if you see a free chair: This is one of the most densely populated countries in the world (16 million people), and table sharing is customary.

There's been a minor revolution in Amsterdam's coffee scene. At one time, if you asked for an ordinary coffee you'd almost invariably be served a watered-down espresso, and a cup of joe to go was uncommon. Now you can find whatever you desire, from iced mochas to soy lattes, in almost every block in the Centrum. **Serious espresso lovers** should check out **de Koffie Salon** (1st Constantijn Huygenstraat 82, map area A7; Utrechtsestraat 130, map area D7). They use Palombini espresso beans that produce a seductive trickle from a vintage hand-pulled Italian machine. **Café Latei** (see below) also makes a great espresso prepared with Sicilian beans. **Al Ponte**, located at the ferry stop IJplein (Amsterdam North), offers espresso with a view. Check out the boat traffic on the IJ waterway, sip an authentic Italian coffee and try their unfathomably good lemon cake. Al Ponte's motto? *Make Coffee Not War!* Sounds good to me. A short, three minute ferry ride from behind Centraal Station.

Koffie verkeerd ("wrong coffee") is a latté. Tea is sometimes charged by the cup, and extra water will be added to the bill. I don't know the reason for this dumb custom. Fresh-squeezed orange juice – commonly referred to in French as *jus d'orange* – is available in most cafés.

Many cafés also serve snacks such as broodjes (small sandwiches) and tostis (usually ham and/or cheese sandwiches squashed into a sandwich toaster). Prices start at about €2.50 for a plain cheese on white roll or *tosti*. Another popular item is apple pie with whipped cream-- a delicious Amsterdam taste experience every visitor should try. **For internet cafés, see the Hanging Out chapter.**

Café Latei - Zeedijk 143, ☎ 625-7485

www.latei.ne

Do you ever wake up and think to yourself: "I feel like drinking a cup of coffee and then buying some organic olive oil and a piece of furniture"? Because this intimate, split-level café's got all that and more. Almost everything in here is for sale: the chair you're sitting on, Finnish wallpaper, '60s Tupperware, knick-knacks, old EPs and Sicilian olive oil. Latei is crammed with bric a brac creating the sensation you're in someone's very ornate living room. It's a great little place to pop into for a fresh-squeezed juice, a big bowl of vegetarian soup or a sandwich made with organic bread. On Thursday, Friday and Saturday nights starting at 18:00 they serve excellent Indian food (vegetarian €8 and €10, organic meat €12) prepared using only fresh ingredients. Open: Mon-Wed 8-18; Thurs-Fri 8-22; Sat 9-22; Sun 11-18. (Map area E4)

Dwaze Zaken - Prins Hendrikkade 50, ☎ 612-4175

www.dwazezaken.nl

I'm not sure why this café is called Foolish Things, because they seem to have it together: changing art exhibitions adorn the space, the food and drinks are yummy, and the bathrooms are spotless. Their terrace is also really nice and if the weather sucks they have comfy couches and chairs inside. A big selection of sandwiches starts at €4, along with soups, wraps, and big salads. Drink-wise they offer delicious tap beer, nice teas, and fresh orange-kiwi-banana juice. In the evenings there's sometimes live music or a spoken-word performance, and then there might be a few euros cover. It's just across the street and to the left of Centraal Station. Open: Tues-Sat 12-24; Sun 12-18. (Map Area E3)

De Tuin - 2e Tuindwarsstraat 13, ☎ 624-4559

De Tuin is a spacious, inviting café in the heart of the Jordaan. It's a traditional "brown café," so called because of the abundance of wood. It's fun to explore this charming neighborhood and then stop here for a drink and a sandwich. The view of the Westerkerk tower from this shopping street is particularly photogenic. Open: Mon-Thurs 10-1; Fri-Sat 10-2; Sun 11-1. (Map area B3)

Café de Pels - Huidenstraat 25, ☎ 622-9037

This is another traditional "brown café" with an authentic Amsterdam ambiance and a diverse clientele. It's warm and welcoming in the winter; in summer the tiny outdoor tables hug this quaint, tiny street, perfect for people watching. Open: Sun-Thurs 10-1; Fri-Sat 10-3. (Map area C5)

Villa Zeezicht - Torensteeg 7, ☎ 626-7433

Often packed, the service here can be a little slow, but Villa Zeezicht remains a cozy café. The seats by the big windows are perfect for reading the paper and people watching. In the summer there are tables outside and on the bridge across the street. Sandwiches start at €3.50. They also offer killer homemade apple pie for €4 – a meal in itself. Make sure to ask for whipped cream. Open: Daily 8-22. (Map area D4)

cafés

Tony's NY City Bagels - Jodenbreestraat 15, ☎ 421-5930; Raadhuisstraat 18, ☎ 638-0186

tonysnycitybagels.

Tony's NY City Bagels offerings don't compare to the real New York doughy delights—but both Amste
dammers and tourists love this place. You can cop an affordable bagel with cream cheese and chives
choose more decadent toppings. They have organic fair-trade coffee with American-style refills for ha
price. Other potables include soups, salads, decent baked goods, espresso, hot chocolate, iced te
fresh juices and shakes. Order your food at the counter, grab a table and they'll bring your grub to yo
A discount card is also available; after nine cups of coffee or nine muffins you get the tenth free. Ope
Mon-Fri 8:30-18; Sat 9-18; Sun 10-18. (Map area E5)

Bagels & Beans

Ferdinand Bolstraat 70, ☎ 672-1610; Keizersgracht 504, ☎ 330-5508; Waterlooplein 2, ☎ 428-8906;
Haarlemmerdijk 122, ☎ 330-4102; Van Baerlestraat 40, ☎ 675-7050

www.bagelsbeans.

Bagels & Beans is a popular Amsterdam bagel chain. Each location has the same menu but uniqu
features; Van Baerlestraat has a pretty garden out back, and Waterlooplein sits market side, gre
for people watching. All the locations offer free WiFi. Bagels with cream cheese start at €2.90, b
there's a big menu offering all sorts of topping combinations—like warm goat cheese-honey-walnut
and-thyme. Jonesing for something sweet? Their warm chocolate muffins rule. Opening times vary b
location but in general they're open daily 8:30-17:30.

Tofani - Kloveniersburgwal 20

Tofani is an unpretentious old-school Italian shop near the Nieuwmarkt selling great sandwiches an
wonderful gelati. Five different hot and cold sandwiches are served on panini bread—like mozzarell
lettuce-tomato-and-basil. Order at the counter and have a seat at one of the tables outside. They'll ta
on the window when it's ready. Open: Mar-Oct only. (Map area E5)

Hanneke's Boom - Dijksgracht 4, ☎ 419-9820

www.hannekesboom.

A brilliant addition to Amsterdam's café scene, Hanneke's Boom (Hanneke's Tree) inhabits a tiny penins
la on the water just east of Centraal Station. This is old school Amsterdam charm at it's best—a relaxe
atmosphere, rough and ready construction style and wholesome food...plus a full bar, of course. The te
race garden is surrounded on three sides by water and small boats can dock. They serve all three mea
here prepared conscious of the "slow food" movement, meaning everything is fresh. €6,50 get's yo
Hanneke's Breakfast: farm fresh yoghurt, a croissant with butter and jam plus coffee or tea. Whatev
time of day you choose to visit, Hanneke's Boom is ready to satisfy your stomach. (Map area: F,G 4.)

Hanneke's Boom

Café Vertigo - Vondelpark 3, ☎ 612-3021

www.vertigo.nl

Vertigo has one of Amsterdam's prettiest and busiest terraces. It's located in the Vondelpark, part of the former Film Museum building. Sitting here is like being in a Victorian painting–only the swarm of rollerbladers, joggers and bicyclists reminds you it's the 21st century. In bad weather you can duck into the cozy low-ceilinged café. On weekends various parties and events happen. Free WiFi. Open: Daily 10-1. (Map area B8)

De Jaren - Nieuwe Doelenstraat 20, ☎ 625-5771

café de jaren.nl

Food here is not special, but I like the spacious-ness, which is unusual in Amsterdam. Summer means two big terraces with a terrific view over the Amstel River. It's near the university and lots of intellectuals hang out reading books or twid-dling with their laptops—free WiFi here. I usually stop in to use the toilet. Located between Wa-terlooplein and Muntplein. Open: Sun-Thurs 10-1; Fri-Sat 10-2. (Map area D6)

De Jaren

Kromhout - Entrepotdok 36, ☎ 330-0929

www.caferestaurantkromhout.nl

Amsterdam has no shortage of charming outdoor, canal-side cafés. But finding one in the Centrum where you're not crammed into a tiny space with traffic whizzing by is another matter. The patio at Kromhout is different. It's spa-cious (for this city), and there's very little traffic except for a steady, entertaining stream of bikes rolling over a little bridge plus the comings and goings of local waterfowl. Whether you're chilling here with a cold beer or having a romantic dinner on a summer night, it's a great spot–situated in a row of historic warehouses. They serve an assortment of sandwiches and salads, as well as more filling meals. The little bottles of organic apple juice they stock are delicious, and they also make excellent coffee. Open: Daily 11-24. (Map area G6)

Skek - Zeedijk 4-8, ☎ 427-0551

www.skek.nl

Skek, a café/bar near Centraal Station on the historic Zeedijk, combines "the culinary with the cultural." They support young, enthusiastic chefs who cook affordable meals made from fresh daily produce. The place is open for lunch and dinner with a diverse menu. Work by new artists is displayed on the walls, and there's a cozy little room up some stairs with a great view of the small stage below where bands, singer/songwriters and upstart jazz cats do their thing weekly, free of charge. Students receive 30% off their meals, all the time. At night the bar gets packed, especially on the weekends. Open: Sun-Thurs 12-1; Fri-Sat 12-3. (Map area E4)

De Badcuyp - 1e Sweelinckstraat 10, ☎ 675-9669

www.badcuyp.nl

Neighborhood activists saved this former bathhouse from demolition. Now De Badcuyp is a "center for art, culture and politics" partly run by volunteers. It's located in the middle of the crowded Albert Cuyp Market (see Markets, Shopping chapter), and in nice weather there are tables outside. Inside it's spacious and relaxed: Newspapers are scattered around and art exhibits line the walls. The upper level gives you a good view of strolling shoppers in the market below. They serve cheap snacks from 11:00 and full meals in the evening from 18 to 22:00. There's often live music, either in the café or in the hall upstairs where they also host popular dance nights featuring salsa, funk, blues, jazz and disco. And once a month they have an open stage. Open: Tues-Thurs 17-1; Fri 17-3; Sat 11-3; Sun 17-1. (Map area E8)

cafés

Manege - Vondelstraat 140, ☎ 618-0942

www.dehollandschemanege.r

I'd always heard this equestrian school had an impressive café with cheap drinks and snacks. It's tru
Walk through the arch under the huge lamps and enter the school via the big doors. The café is throug
the door on the left and up a grandiose stairway. There's a balcony with tables overlooking the trainin
area, but if you find the horsey aroma a bit much, you can still see through the windows of the café
main room. It was formerly very elegant and is now filled with cats. If you're coming from Vondelpar
take the exit near the Film Museum. Vondelstraat runs alongside the park. (See Parks, Hanging Ou
chapter). Open: Mon-Fri 14-23 (Wed open at 10); Sat 10-17; Sun 10-17. (Map area A7)

Manege

East of Eden - Linnaeusstraat 11A, ☎ 665-0743

This spacious café sits opposite the Tropenmuseum (see Museum chapter) and near the Dapper ma
ket (see Shopping chapter). Seating is a mish-mash of couches and easy chairs. Light streams throug
the high windows on two sides--warm and mellow in the winter. Summers you can sit out on th
sunny terrace. Open: Sun-Thurs 11-1; Fri-Sat 11-2. (Map area H7)

De Roos (The Rose) - PC Hooftstraat 183 (entrance in Vondelpark), ☎ 689-5477

www.roos.r

Folks into "creative and spiritual growth" or alternative health care might dig De Roos. It's located
a Victorian style house at the edge of Vondelpark, home to a new-age shop, practitioners' rooms an
a tearoom. A lunch menu is offered daily from 12 to16:00, including affordable soups, sandwiche
salads, homemade cakes and pastries. Drinks are also low-priced-- one of the best deals in this rit
neighborhood. On weekdays, dinner is served from 17:30 to 20:00. Order downstairs then head up
the plant-filled solarium, where classical music floats in from the adjacent shop. Tea-room open: Mo
Fri 9:30-20; Sat-Sun 9:30-16. (Map area B7)

Café Restaurant Noorderlicht - NDSM Werf, T.T. Neveritaweg 15, Amsterdam North,
☎ 065-059-0958

www.noorderlichtcafe.

The original boat like version of north Amsterdam's Noorderlicht was cute as hell – until it burned rig
down to the ground. It's been rebuilt and encased in a transparent shell; nice and warm in winter an

easy to open in summer. Located at the happening NDSM Wharf (see Music chapter) this spot has a fantastic view over the Ij waterway and the industrial terrain. Reasonably priced Tostis, sandwiches, uitsmijters and daily specials are all available plus a full bar. Also, expect to encounter live music, art exhibitions and sundowner parties. Open: Sun-Tues-Thurs 11-23; Fri-Sat 11-1.

Café de Molli - Van Ostadestraat 55, ☎ 676-1427

www.molli.nl

This volunteer-run café with an emphasis on politics is in a building squatted over 30 years ago. Molli frequently hosts theme nights with videos and speakers on subjects such as genetically-modified food or the role of Shell Oil (those murdering motherfuckers) in Nigeria. They serve super-cheap meals (see Restaurants, Food chapter) but you need to call after 15:00 to reserve. Drinks are very cheap. Tea is free. Benefits and parties featuring discussions, Folk-Punk bands and vegan eats happen here frequently—check their site for details. Open: Daily 21-1.

The Lonely Collective Day Café (at Joe's Garage) - Pretoriusstraat 43

www.joesgarage.nl

Joe's Garage, one of the few remaining active squats in the once heavily occupied east Amsterdam Oosterpark neighborhood, has a special café on Wednesdays for like minded folks who "...are lonely but prefer to spend their loneliness collectively." From 14-18:00, you can drink coffee, eat pastries, surf the internet, socialize, veg or even bake a cake. The LCDC even encourages guests to "...read the news or latest propaganda while sitting on the loo," if they so desire. Sounds like my house.

Backstage Boutique and Coffee Corner - Utrechtsedwarsstraat 67, ☎ 622 3638

Greg, one of the Christmas Twins (identical twins that were big stars back in the US), died some years back, and he is still missed. But his brother Gary is still running the Pee Wee-esque café they built to-gether, and its unique atmosphere endures. This place is great! They serve coffees, teas, juices and an assortment of sandwiches and cakes. The bottom of the menu proclaims: "Mama wanted girls!" The walls are decorated with wild sweaters and hats that were designed and made by the twins. If you're lucky, you might even walk out with a souvenir postcard. Open: Mon-Sat 10-17:30. (Map area E7)

Cannabis

Coffeeshops are an integral part of Amsterdam culture, a place where you can peacefully partake of some of the world's finest types of weed and hashish. Tourists visit en masse to sample smoke, chill out, listen to some tunes and soak in the vibes. The current xenophobic, backward-thinking right wing Dutch government passed a bill through Parliament allowing only Dutch citizens, registered smokers, to visit coffeeshops. Fortunately, it is being delayed, at least until 2015. Some cannabis culture experts and businesspeople predict the bill will never come into law, and if it does it won't be enforced.

So don't worry folks! You can still walk into an Amsterdam coffeeshop, order an espresso and a joint, sit back and puff, listen to music, perhaps have a game of backgammon or chess – without worrying about being arrested.

Almost all coffeeshops have a menu listing the types of smoke available, where each one is from or how it's grown. It's fun to try grass and hash from different parts of the world, but the *nederwiet* (Dutch grown indoor) normally gets you the most blasted. Prices are usually listed by the gram, but the weed is sometimes sold in set-price bags of €10. Many coffeeshops will also let you buy smaller amounts. Don't be afraid to ask to see the menu: It's there to make choosing easy.

Some strains are listed as "hydro," meaning they were grown hydroponically. Others are listed as "bio," meaning they were grown in soil. Note that "bio" in this case doesn't mean organically grown, as it does with bio products in grocery stores. However, many coffeeshops are starting to sell organically-grown strains and may list these as bio as well. If you're in doubt, just ask. It's also no problem to ask to see the buds before you buy. Then relax, roll yourself a number or hit a bong and ponder the absurdity of North America and Europe's repressive and hypocritical "War on Drugs," and how fantastic it is to be openly smoking in Amsterdam!

The weed here can be a lot stronger than what you're used to back home, depending on your smoking experience. Even veterans who go one toke over the line get the cold sweats. If you find that a friend of yours is too high, feels a bit sick, or is about to pull a whitey, a sweet drink (like orange juice or cola) will help bring him or her back. Coffeeshop employees are usually helpful returning your comrade to an upright position. Just thought I'd mention that.

In spite of what some of the tackier shops in the tourist areas might try to imply, you don't have to buy weed every time you visit a coffeeshop, though you should buy something – at least a drink or some munchies.

Attention: Don't buy anything on the street! You will definitely be ripped off!

Warning: Space cakes and bonbons containing grass or hash are sold in some coffeeshops. They can be very strong, almost like tripping, so have fun but be prepared for a long, intense high. Also keep in mind that they can take up to a couple of hours to kick in, so don't gobble down another one because you don't feel anything right away...............What?

solar pipe hits with a magnifying glass

TOUCH EXHIBIT

"FEEL THE HEMP"

coffeeshops

Grey Area - Oude Leliestraat 2, ☎ 420-4301
www.greyarea.nl

This tiny shop is world-renowned for selling exclusive weed strains like Silver Bubble and Martian Mean Green plus the legendary Grey Crystal unpressed hash. It's American owned with a friendly staff that'll gladly let you check out the buds and offer advice like which smoke is uplifting and which fossilizes you. They have a bong bar, free of charge, with choice pieces from ROOR and a Volcano vaporizer. Prices range across the spectrum, but the buds are killer and they give deals – including 1/8ths offered in ziplock baggies. Grey Area gets packed with lines sometimes stretching out the door, but don't be discouraged: the tasty smokeables are worth the wait. Open: Daily 12-20. (Map area C4)

Amnesia - Herengracht 133, ☎ 427-7874

Situated on a beautiful central canal, Amnesia is a welcoming shop with a splendid sidewalk terrace in warm weather. A friendly staff, a big menu and quality music make this a nice place to have a smoke break while strolling the famous *Jordaan* neighborhood. You can drink a big latte and smoke a spliff while grooving to vintage ska and reggae or perhaps some ambient drum and bass. Or vapor yourself with one of their house vaporizers. Open: Daily 9-1. (Map area C4)

X-large vaporizer hit at Amnesia

Basjoe - Kloveniersburgwal 62, ☎ 627-3858

If you're feeling like a lazy afternoon spent smoking joints, listening to reggae or funk and lounging with a beautiful Amsterdam canal view, then Basjoe's the place. The interior is comfortable and the dudes who run this place are cool and hospitable. They also make an amazing mixed-fruit shake—it takes a few minutes, but believe me this yummy vitamin kick is worth it. Besides, you'll be so chilled out that you won't mind. Open Sun-Thurs 10-1; Fri-Sat 10-2. (Map area D5) cannabis

The Rookies - Korte Leidsedwarsstraat 145, ☎ 639-0978

www.rookies.n

Though The Rookies has a neighborhood-bar feel to it, it draws an international crowd. This is partly due to its long-standing reputation for being tourist-friendly and for selling good weed and hash, but also because many of the guests from Hotel Rookies (see Places to Sleep chapter) make the coffeeshop their home base while in Amsterdam. It's a great spot to kick back, sample the wares and meet other travellers. The shop is well equipped to meet smokers' needs: It was the first coffeeshop in town to sell pure joints, and they have bongs and a vaporizer available for use – just ask at the bar. Since the tobacco smoking ban they've built a plexiglass wall separating the bar (pure weed only) and an adjacent room (tobacco and mixed spliffs). This lessened the Rookies atmosphere but you can smoke what you want and remain indoors. In nice weather you can sit out front. Open: Sun-Thurs 10-00:45; Fri-Sat 10 2:45. (Map area C7)

De Rokerij - Lange Leidsedwarsstraat 41, ☎ 622-9442

www.rokerij.ne

De Rokerij is a beautifully decorated coffeeshop selling quality smokables located in one of Amsterdam's tackier tourist strips. The decor is a mixture of Indian and Nepali motifs with comfortable nooks to settle into while you enjoy herbal refreshment and dig the well selected, spacey music. It's a popular spot–especially nights and weekends. My only complaints are pricey drinks and their refusal to allow baseball caps – or any sort of headgear – in their shops… that's wack. Open: Sun-Thurs 10-1; Fri-Sat 'til 3. (Map area C7)

De Rokerij - Singel 8, ☎ 422-6643

This Rokerij is one of the nicest coffeeshops in the Centraal Station area. There are African influenced murals on the walls and low cushioned seats that make the asses of flatbacks like me fall asleep–try to grab the padded benches near the door if your booty challenged. (For the record, there are also other Rokerijs at Elandsgracht 53 and Amstel 8). Singel branch open: Sun-Thurs 9-1; Fri-Sat 'til 2. (Map area D3,

Dampkring - Handboogstraat 29 / Haarlemmerstraat 44, ☎ 638- 0705

www.dampkring.n

Long before scenes for Ocean's 12 were filmed here, the super-funky décor, including walls like melted candle wax, and some killer hash and buds made the Dampkring a favorite with both locals and tourists. This joint gets packed and if you're looking for a mellow experience the music can be a little loud, otherwise it's a comfortable place with a friendly staff. The new Haarlemmerstraat location is a three storey shop with spacey/chic décor and an amazing neighborhood view from the loungey upstairs room. Unfortunately, they enforce the ever-increasing lame no hats or headbands policy. Their extensive menu (which they sell as a souvenir) details what type of high you can expect from each of the various strains and includes information on their fair-trade policies. Fair-trade cannabis! Only in Amsterdam. Open: Mon-Thurs 10-1; Fri-Sat 10-2; Sun 11-1. (Map area C6) (Haarlemmerstraat: Map area D3)

Tweede Kamer - Heisteeg 6, ☎ 422-2236

This sweet little jazzy coffeeshop–dark wooden interior, deep red curtains–has the same great menu as the Dampkring. Though the space is small, the shop feels comfortable. The staff is patient and informative with tourists who need a little time to make up their minds. That's cool. Open: Mon-Sat 10-1; Sun 11-1. (Map area D5)

Siberië - Brouwersgracht 11, ☎ 623-5909

www.siberie.ne

Siberië is a neighborhood coffeeshop catering to a local and international crowd who appreciate the art exhibitions, cool tunes and terrific smoke variety in all price ranges. They have inexpensive drinks, a friendly staff and a computer to check e-mails. Be sure to make time for a stroll along the gorgeous canal where Siberië is located. Five minutes walk from Centraal Station. Open: Sun-Thurs 11-23; Fri-Sat 11-24. (Map area D3)

de Republiek - 2e Nassaustraat 1a, ☎ 682-8431

www.republiek.net

De Republiek, with connections to Siberië (see above) and Ruigoord (see Festivals, Music chapter), is an institution in this west-side neighborhood. They've been around for ages, and locals are always dropping by for a smoke and a chat. It's not as busy as Siberië and therefore a little more restful. Upstairs you can check your e-mail. There's also a large assortment of teas, including fresh mint and yogi, and delicious coffee. Open: Sun 10-23; Mon-Thurs 9-22; Fri-Sat 9-24. (Map area B2)

Katsu - 1e Van Der Helststraat 70, ☎ 675-2617

www.katsu.nl

Katsu is a long-standing neighborhood coffeeshop located just off the Albert Cuyp Market in De Pijp. It's got a shabby, homey feel to it, and some wicked grass. They're famous for their Haze #1, with a wonderful soaring high. Their hash, made with the Ice-O-Later (see Pollinator Co, Shopping chapter), is out of this world. Drinks are reasonably priced, there's a vaporizer, the music is good, and they have a pinball machine. Well worth a visit. Open: Mon-Thurs 11-23; Fri-Sat 11-24; Sun 12-23.

de Supermarkt - Frederik Hendrikstraat 69, ☎ 486-2497

www.desupermarkt.net

This is another shop in the same family as Siberië and Republiek, but a bit off the beaten track. De Supermarket offers the same products and the same reasonable drink prices. There's a big wood table at the front that's warm when the afternoon sun spills in, a tranquil spot to smoke and read a magazine. Hanging by the counter is a diploma certifying that the staff successfully completed the Cannabis College's "basic cannabis knowledge." Open: Daily 10-23. (Map area A4)

YoYo - 2e Jan v.d. Heijdenstraat 79, ☎ 664-7173

YoYo is a perfect place to spend a mellow afternoon reading or writing while you slowly smoke a joint or two. The shop is spacious and airy, and in warm weather there's a terrace on a car-free street. You won't find big frosty mega-buds here, but the weed is organically grown and produces a satisfying, mellow high. As it's a bit out of the center (near Albert Cuyp Market), their prices are low. Buds are sold in €5 and €10 bags. And they might be the cheapest coffeeshop for food and drinks. Open: Mon-Sat 12-19; Sun 16-19. (Map area E8)

La Tertulia - Prinsengracht 312, ☎ 623-8503

www.coffeeshopamsterdam.com

Plants, flowers and a little fountain give this coffeeshop a tropical feeling but if it's not raining, La Tertulia's outdoor terrace is superb. Flowers adorn all the canal side tables where you can relax, check the crazy bike traffic and puff at your leisure. This building is easy to find: it's covered with a Van Gogh style sunflower mural. Open: Tues-Sat 11-19. (Map area C5)

420 Café - Oudebrugsteeg 27, ☎ 623-4848

www.420cafe.com

Classic rock dominates the sound system here and freakier folks will like hearing regularly played Zappa tunes—or checking the giant poster of Frank clad in Dutch football colors. 420 Café is clean, comfortable and has Amsterdam's friendliest coffeeshop staff-- they don't even mind if you eat take-out food here. They offer a good smoke selection and it's one of those places where it's always 4:20. Open: Sun-Thurs 12-1; Fri-Sat 12-3. (Map area D4)

Paradox - 1e Bloemdwarsstraat 2, ☎ 623-5639

www.paradoxamsterdam.demon.nl

Not only can you buy and smoke cannabis at this wee shop, but you can satisfy your munchies, as well. Paradox serves up delicious food and is known for awesome fruit shakes. A banana/strawberry shake costs €3.90, fresh squeezed orange juice €2.50. They also cook up homemade soup and veggie burgers. Located in Amsterdam's beautiful *Jordaan* neighborhood. Open: Daily 10-20, but note that the kitchen closes at 16:00. (Map area B4)

Dutch Flowers - Singel 387, ☎ 624-7624

www.dutch-flowers.nl

Dutch Flowers, located in the city center by Spui Circle, has a unique canal view and the bike/pedestrian traffic through a bustling adjacent alley is a people watching paradise. If your stoney head needs printed distraction, a stack of magazines and comics is available. Their good selection of weed and hash is also sold in small amounts. Open: Sun-Thurs 10-1; Fri-Sat 'til 2. (Map area C6)

Any Day - Korte Kolksteeg 5, ☎ 420-8698

The first time I visited this tiny coffeeshop the guy behind the counter welcomed a friend and me with a vaporizer hit--before we even had our coats off! Now that's friendly service. For hash heads, a quality selection of clean Morrocan hashhish is available at a fair price. It's not far from Centraal Station and caters to a local and international crowd. Across the street there's a brothel with girls in the windows. Open: Daily 10-1. (Map area D3)

Kadinsky - Rosmarijnsteeg 9, ☎ 624-7023

www.channels.nl/kadinsky.html

This hip coffeeshop is a perfect spot to kick back and smoke your first spliff of the day. Music varies from rock to reggae to Sinatra – depending on who's working. They've got great discounts on their extensive smoke menu if you buy 5 grams. Delicious cookies and organic apple juice are also on hand. It's located on a little street near the Spui, and Kadinsky also has tiny shops at Langebrugsteeg 7 and Zoutsteeg 14. Open: Daily 10-1. (Map area D5)

The Bluebird - Sint Antoniesbreestraat 71, ☎ 622-5232

www.coffeeshopbluebird.nl

The huge old menu at the Bluebird was famous for its variety and the creative way it was displayed—a thick, three ring binder with page upon page of weed and hash stuffed baggies. Current laws (see below) have forced them to cut back some on the breadth of the selection, but the quality of their wares remains high. One problem is the shop gets uncomfortably packed—try to grab a terrace seat outside. Open: Daily 9:30-1. (Map area E5)

Greenhouse - Oudezijds Voorburgwal 191, ☎ 627-1739

www.greenhouse.org

Little lights embedded in the walls gradually change color, and the ceiling, tables and washroom walls are encrusted with sea shells. I'm not sure whether it's the decor or the good weed that draws them, but the list of celebrities who've visited this popular shop keeps growing. Sometimes it gets too crowded, but mostly it's an agreeable place to while away some time, especially if you can snag a seat out front. If you like their weed you can buy their seeds at the Greenhouse Seed Company (Langebrugsteeg 13). A new roomier Greenhouse is open on Haarlemmerstraat with a fish tank under the see-through floor, Egyptian style hieroglyphic wall art and a wide breakfast and lunch menu. Open: Sun-Thurs 9-1; Fri-Sat 9-3 (Map area D5)

Homegrown Fantasy - Nieuwezijds Voorburgwal 87, ☎ 627-5683

www.homegrownfantasy.com

Homegrown Fantasy is an old school internationally renowned coffeeshop. A few years ago they almost lost their lease—and the doors nearly shut for good. Luckily for you, stoney people, this airy, art filled gallery/coffeeshop is still in business. Enjoy a spliff, a pot of mint tea or a huge café latte, sit by the panomamic side window and peep the steady foot traffic. Or challenge your mate to a game of chess, if you're not too high. The bathrooms are super spacey complete with black lights that make your pee look like glowing milk. Open: Daily 10-24. (Map area D4)

The Otherside - Reguliersdwarsstraat 6, ☎ 421-1014

www.theotherside.nl

The Otherside is located in one of Amsterdam's main gay streets. They have a full menu, a friendly staff and it's easy to meet people here, locals and tourists alike. It's a cool spot to smoke a spliff and check the pedestrian traffic out of their big front window. The only drawback is the sometimes-blaring dance music. Open: Daily 11-1. (Map area D6)

Tweedy - Vondelstraat 104, ☎ 618 0344

www.tweedy.nl

Tweedy sits near Vondelpark across the street from the Vondel Church. It's a pleasant place to get stoned, especially sitting in one of the three train compartment booths, complete with magazine and board game stuffed overhead luggage racks. They also have a pool table and a good selection of candy bars. Open: Daily 11-24. (Map area A7)

Barney's - Reguliersgracht 27, Haarlemmerstraat 102

www.barneys.biz

While I like the original Barney's on Haarlemmerstraat, when I want to smoke a jay and chill I head for this newer branch. The space features soothing colors on the walls, comfortable chairs and Volcano vaporizers. They sell the same high quality buds, like Utopia Haze and Blue Cheese, here like Barney's other locations, plus the usual assortment of coffees, juices and shakes – but no food. There is also a giant screen on one wall – nice if you like to get high while watching films or World Cup football games. Open: Daily 9-1 (Map area D7) (Haarlemmerstraat: D3)

Abraxas - Jonge Roelensteeg 12, ☎ 625-5763

www.abraxasparadise.nl

The three floors of this old house each have their own unique style and ambience. Sitting in the uppermost room feels like visiting an elf's treehouse. The second floor has lots of couches for lounging about; the ground floor an Arabian-style chill room and computers with free internet access. Abraxas serves the usual assortment of drinks, plus hash shakes, hash coffee, and weed tea. Several DJs work here, so the music is usually interesting. Open: Daily 10-1 (in summer 9-1). (Map area D5)

De Overkant Hortus - Nieuwe Herengracht 71, ☎ 620-6577

De Overkant is located right across the canal from the Botanical Gardens (see Museums chapter) and close to the Waterlooplein market (see Shopping chapter). It's a small shop with a simple, uncluttered interior – so simple, in fact, there aren't any chairs! Guess they don't want anyone hanging around too long. But smoking a joint here and then exploring the Gardens is a great way to spend an afternoon. Open: Daily 10-24. (Map area F6)

Dolphins - Kerkstraat 39, ☎ 625-9162

This split-level shop sells its wares in small paper bags that read: "This bag is earth and dolphin friendly" and "Don't mix this with alcohol!" There's free WiFi and you can smoke mixed spliffs or cigarettes in the downstairs den. Upstairs is pure weed and hash only. The music can be a bit too Top-40 for my taste, but this is a good shop for a clean piece of Moroccan hash or a quick smoke while in the Leidseplein area. Open: Sun-Thurs 10-1, Fri-Sat 10-3 (Map area C6)

Happy Feelings - Kerkstraat 51, ☎ 639-1154

www.happyfeelingsamsterdam.nl

Happy Feelings is Amsterdam's first automated coffeeshop. Machines with drinks (chocolate milk €1.50, coffee €2.00) are set against the back wall, and even papers are sold out of a machine. The dealer, however, is real and although the menu can vary in quality, tasty smoke like NYC Diesel is also available. He'll gladly let you have a look at the buds and the bags are weighed to order. Although this shop is centrally located, it's a family-run business and has an unpretentious feel. If you need a break from the bustling Leidsestraat, Happy Feelings is a nice stop. Open daily: 13-1 (Map area C 6,7)

Amsterdam Coffeeshop Directory

www.coffeeshop.freeuk.com

With over 1000 pages of info about Amsterdam's soft drug scene, this website is a great place to find out more info about the coffeeshops I recommend, as well as many others. It's been online since 1998 and features photos, reviews, maps and more.

seeds and grow shops

There are numerous reputable seed shops around town, but also a lot of fly-by-night companies selling inferior products. The best companies have spent years developing their strains in order to produce a stable, reliable seed. I've listed a few of them below. **Remember:** It's legal to buy cannabis seeds in the Netherlands but importing them to most other countries is illegal.

T.H.Seeds - Nieuwendijk 13, ☎ 421-1762

www.thseeds.com

Hemp Works (see Hemp Stores, below) sells its own in-house line, T.H.Seeds. They've been in business since 1993 and are well respected amongst growers in the know. Strains available include the incredible Sage 'n Sour, Kushage, Rambo and their delicious resiny MK Ultra. Make your purchase during their 4:20 happy hour, mention *Get Lost!* and get 10% off! Open: Daily 12-19. (Map area D3)

Sensi Seed Bank - Oudezijds Achterburgwal 150, ☎ 624-0386

www.sensiseeds.com

This legendary seed bank, original purveyors of strains like Big Bud and NL/Haze, is a mecca for DIY gardening. Every growing essential is on sale here, starting with seeds. Some of the seed prices may seem a bit high, but they have proven genetic quality, attracting a slew of professional growers. Sensi Seeds are often winners at the Cannabis Cup Awards (see below). You can also purchase seeds at their museum, and at their new shop (the old Sensi coffeeshop) nearby on Oude Doelenstraat 20. They also have a small outlet near Centraal Station at Nieuwendijk 26. Open: daily 10-23. (Map area E5)

DNA - Sint Nicolaasstraat 41, ☎ 778-7220

www.dnagenetics.com

DNA (Don 'N' Aaron) has earned a reputation as one of Amsterdam's premier breeders. Along with notorious cannabis strains like Martian Mean Green and L.A. Confidential they stock several other outstanding seed varieties. The centrally located shop is a welcoming place with a curved bar-style counter and a fresh-water fish tank built into the back wall. Besides seeds DNA sells T-shirts, hoodies, hemp caps and various bongs and glass pipes. You can drop by and have a chat or a smoke – these guys are seriously knowledgeable about their award-winning strains. Dry crystal extraction has kept the boys busy experimenting with the sweetest smelling, intensely powerful unpressed hash. Flashlight vaporizing is a new way to smoke said hash and at DNA they're busy perfecting the style. I was fortunate enough to try some limited edition Kandy Kush crystals—which gave me a cinematic high. With a good attitude and a pair of sunglasses handy, you just might get a taste. Flashlight vaporizing is bright as an exploding star, which is why you need shades! If you're really lucky you'll get to try some of Don's mom's vegan potato salad to cure your munchies. Yum! Open: Daily 12-6. (Map area D4)

Pollinator Company - Nieuwe Herengracht 25, ☎ 470-8889

www.pollinator.nl

This impressive shop caters to almost all your pre- and post-harvest needs, but their specialty is hash-ish manufacturing. Owner Mila Jansen invented the Pollinator, the Ice-O-Lator and newest to the list --The Bubble-ator, the ultimate tool for cold-water crystal extraction. It's un-fucking-believable how this simple-to-use device makes such fine hash from marijuana shake and other plant discards. She's also selected top grade seeds--some of the world's best -hash making strains--also available here. Cool. Inside the door on your right (and on-line) is the Hall of Fame, a hash display with entries from around the world. They also sell books, hemp products, smoking accessories, vaporizers, and – as the space is shared by the Botanic Herbalist – psychoactive plants (see Smart Shops, Shopping chapter). Open: Mon 12-19; Tues-Fri 11-19; Sat 12-19. (Map area E6)

Sagarmatha Seeds

www.highestseeds.com

This company's motto, "highest on earth," refers in part to their name: Sagarmatha means Mount Everest in Nepalese. The 100% organically-produced, selective genetic seeds they sell are aimed at connoisseurs who appreciate delicious results-- tasty seed strains like Bubbleberry and Yumbolt. Check their site for more information.

Soma Seeds

www.somaseeds.nl

Over the years, I've smoked several weed varieties grown from Soma's organically-bred seeds – absolutely delicious. They're available on-line and around town at places like the Seed Boutique (see below).

The Flying Dutchmen - Oudezijds Achterburgwal 131, ☎ 428-4023

www.flyingdutchmen.com

The Flying Dutchmen sells its seeds from an easy-going shop located in the Red Light District across the canal from the Cannabis College (see box). You can choose from the house line, or from one of many other companies' products. And check out their impressive selection of glass pipes. Open: Daily 11-19. (Map area E5)

hemp stores

Hemp Works - Nieuwendijk 13, ☎ 421-1762

www.hempworks.nl

Hemp Works sell designer clothing called "industrial organic wear." Most of the clothes in stock – jeans, dresses, shirts, hoodies and more – carry their own label and include unique touches like their patented sewn-in rolling-paper dispensers. Their popular winter coat, The HoodLamb, even has secret-stash, iPod, and PSP pockets. (Snoop Dog has one, but his is bulletproof.) Hemp skate-shoes from IPATH are available here, made entirely of sustainable materials with bonus features like coconut honeycomb soles and stash pockets. Other labels stocked here include KanaBeach, Livity, and Hemp Valley. They also sell a wide variety of hand-blown glass pipes, grinders, and a choice selection of knick-knacks that make good gifts for discerning smokers back home. Open: Daily 12-19. (Map area D3)

Pollinator Company - Nieuwe Herengracht 25, ☎ 470-8889

www.pollinatorcompany.com

Pollinator Company is unique in its wide array of products. As if all the other great stuff available here isn't enough (see Grow Shops, above), they also stock hemp items: food (try the delicious hemp-burger mix), oils, clothing from Euro-American Marketing (www.hemp-amsterdam.com), and lots more. Open: Mon-Sat 11-20. (Map area E6)

Hempshopper - Nieuwezijds Voorburgwal 80, Singel 10; ☎ 528-5556

www.hempshopper.com

Hempshopper has crammed everything associated with hemp and cannabis into one shop, with a vast selection of seeds, clothes, soap, papers, tea, backpacks, literature, lollipops – the list is endless – on sale here in this hemp-shopper's mini-emporium. The Nieuwezijds location is quite small and filled to the rafters like a green version of some stuffed Turkish market stall. The guys who run this place are cool and informative. Both shops are centrally located. Singel: Open: Daily 10-22; Nieuwezijds: Open Mon-Fri 10-20; Sat-Sun 10-22. (Map area: D4, D3)

headshops

The Headshop - Kloveniersburgwal 39, ☎ 624-9061

www.headshop.nl

Lots of establishments in this central neighborhood call themselves headshops, but this is the real deal. It's been in business since 1968 and stocks a myriad of pipes, bongs, papers, books, magazines, postcards, stickers and the required collection of incense and Indian clothing. They have a good reputation—reflected by the sometimes swarming crowds. Open: Mon-Sat 11-18. (Map area E5)

Baba Souvenir Shop - Warmoesstraat 47, ☎ 428-2504

www.babashops.com

This is a clean, well-stocked shop full of drug paraphernalia, hemp accessories, books and more. Everything is nicely displayed, including a wide assortment of glass pipes. Open: Daily 9-22:30 (Map area E4)

ROOR Shop - Sint Nikolasstraat 19, ☎ 330-2681

www.roor-shop-amsterdam.com

Not exactly a headshop, more like a pristine glass water-pipe emporium, ROOR is Amsterdam's Shangri-la for bong heads. One whole wall is devoted to showing their unique, handblown smoking pieces—color coordinated logos and mirrors enhance this impressive display. They also sell select cannabis seeds, including the limited edition Howard Marks "Mr Nice" line. You can rent pieces here and have your own bong —portable and protected with a carrying bag–while coffeeshop hopping. Unique non-smoking gifts are also available like beautiful custom-made glass baby bottles. Located in the same tiny alley as DNA (see cannabis, seeds), near the Nieuwedijk shopping street. (Map area D4)

cannabis competitions

High Times Cannabis Cup - Third week of November

www.cannabiscup.com

If you're visiting Amsterdam during American Thanksgiving week (the prizes are awarded on Thanksgiving night), check out the Cannabis Cup Awards. High Times magazine hosts this annual marijuana harvest festival. It's mainly an American affair celebrating Dutch weed-growers with several days of cannabis-related events culminating in the actual awards given for best grass and hash strains, best seed companies, and best coffeeshops. Related parties happen around town every night, often with hot bands or hip hop acts playing, and an award ceremony grand finale at the Melkweg. There's also a

Hemp Expo definitely worth a visit. Judges' passes bought in advance are around $200 US, but cheap day-passes to the Expo are also available – well worth it for the amount of free smoke on offer. I scored a tasty nugget of the Chiesel at a previous cup, two months before its coffeeshop debut!

High Life International Hemp Fair - Mid-January

www.highlife.nl

This annual celebration of all things cannabis has been around for more than 15 years. And it's big: The three-day hemp fair has been held at the giant RAI convention center (Europaplein 22) with thousands of visitors and over 100 booths from a dozen countries. The High Life awards, given to coffeeshops and seed companies for the best weed and hash, happen on the first night – and then it's party time.

420 Grower & Breeder Cup - April 18,19... and 20 (of course)

www.icmag.com/ic

The G&B Cup is an evolving event with more participants and greater improvements each year. Growers and breeders are the main focus, rather than seed companies and coffeeshops, but the three-day event also includes parties and entertainment. Judging passes cost €215 to €255, which apparently come with a shitload of weed for your personal edification, and there are day passes available for €30.

a note on drugs in Amsterdam

Concerning cannabis, Holland leads the western world in progressive thinking and action: Soft drugs like grass and hashish have been decriminalized for more than three decades. Small amounts of these can be bought, sold, and consumed without police interference.

Trafficking in hard drugs is dealt with seriously, but addiction is considered a matter of health and social welfare rather than a criminal or law-enforcement problem. The number of addicts in Holland – where they can receive treatment without fear of criminal prosecution – is much lower than in other countries where the law is used to strip people of their human rights (not to mention their property).

Along with the U.S., some European Union member states demand Dutch conformity to their own repressive drug laws. This has resulted in new drug policies that, while still more liberal than elsewhere, reflect a regressive trend in the Dutch authorities' thinking.

The Cannabis College (O.Z. Achterburgwal 124; 423-4420; *www.cannabiscollege.com*) is a non-profit organization formed to educate the public about all the cannabis plant's uses. Volunteers who run the college are dedicated to ending insane and unreasonable punishments inflicted world wide on those who choose, for whatever reason, to use cannabis. They're located in a traditional 17th-century canal house. Stop in to look at the exhibits and see what events are happening. If you want to visit their beautiful basement garden they ask for a €2.50 suggested donation, used to help fund their work. Open: Daily 11-19, and possibly longer in summer, shorter in winter. (Map area D5)

Shopping

Stores in parts of Amsterdam designated as "tourist areas" – most of the Centrum– are now allowed to open on Sundays. Some, however, still hold to tradition and lock their doors from 17 or 18:00 on Saturday until after lunch on Monday. Thursday night is koopavond – shopping evening – in Amsterdam, and the streets and stores are bustling 'til 21:00.

Areas particularly popular with shopaholics are: the Kalverstraat & Nieuwendijk – car-free and crowded with big chain stores (map area D5-4); the *Negen Straatjes* (Nine Streets, map area C5) – nine charming little streets filled with small independent boutiques; and the Haarlemmerstraat & Haarlemmerdijk (map area C2-3), just west of Centraal Station – pleasant, busy, and full of shops and cafés.

markets

Albert Cuypmarkt - Albert Cuypstraat (between Ferdinand Bolstraat & Van Woustraat)
www.albertcuypmarkt.com

The biggest and arguably the best, Amsterdam's most famous market is crowded with stalls and shoppers. You'll find everything from fruit and veggies to clothes and hardware. There's one stall selling warm, freshly made *stroopwafels*, a thin, chewy, syrupy cookie of love – the ultimate sweet Dutch experience. Blank CDs are cheap here. Underwear is a good deal, and so are plain cotton T-shirts (if yours are getting smelly). At many of the stalls you don't pick your own fruit and some vendors are assholes, routinely slipping one or two rotting pieces into each bag. This happens to both tourists and Dutch shoppers, so don't take it personally and don't be afraid to complain. To pick your own produce shop at the Turkish, Morrocan, and Surinamese shops found around most market areas. Open: Mon-Sat 9-16. (Map area E8)

Organic Farmers' Market - Noordermarkt
www.boerenmarktamsterdam.nl

The Organic Farmers' Market is open on Saturdays from 9 to 16:00. Its location at the foot of the Noorderkerk (North Church, Map area C3) lends a medieval feel to this fantastic organic market. The booths sell healthy produce, delicious bread, used records, second-hand clothing, bric-a-brac, books and antiques. There's a playground for kids and an organic pancake stand to keep their little bellies full. Top rate street musicians often perform, adding extra ambience. Right around the corner, on the same day, is the Lindengracht market (see below). Another Saturday organic market takes place in the Nieuwmarkt (see Public Squares, Hanging Out chapter) from 9 to 16:00.

Lindenmarkt - Lindengracht

This all-purpose market is a bit more expensive than Albert Cuyp but still has some good deals. Located in a beautiful neighborhood around the corner from the Organic Farmers' Market (see above). An easy way to get to this and the Noordermarkt is the *Opstapper* mini-bus from Centraal Station, Waterlooplein, or anywhere along the Prinsengracht (see Public Transport, Getting Around chapter). Open: Sat 9-15. (Map area C3)

Noordermarkt - Noordermarkt

This is the ideal Monday morning bargain hunting destination for die-hard shoppers – new and used clothes, books, records, antiques and bric-a-brac galore. After it closes you can find good stuff left on the street. And just for the record, there have been markets at this location since 1627. Open: Mon 9-14. (Map area C3)

Dappermarkt - Dapperstraat

Dappermarkt is Amsterdam's version of a multicultural, neighborhood bazaar–African, Asian, Middle Eastern, South American and Dutch. This all-purpose outdoor market is Amsterdam's cheapest and highest rated. Tasty falafels are sold at an Egyptian stall and cheap snacks—french fries, fried fish and Vietnamese spring rolls—are readily available. It's close to Oosterpark (see Parks, Hanging Out chapter), the Tropenmuseum (see Museum chapter), and the windmill (see IJ Brewery, Bars chapter). Open: Mon-Sat 9-16. (Map area H7)

Ten Kate Market - Ten Katestraat

If you're a more adventurous tourist and end up exploring the West Amsterdam area, pay a visit to this lively neighborhood market. Kinkerstraat, the main shopping street running perpendicular to Ten Katestraat, lacks charm, but the streets and canals behind the market are pretty. It's near the Kashmir Lounge (see Bars chapter) and the sublime Planet Rose (see Restaurants). Open: Mon-Sat 9-17. (Map area A6)

Ten Katemarkt

Waterlooplein Market - Waterlooplein

Waterlooplein has a terrific flea market where you can find new/used clothing, jewellery, turntables spray paint and all kinds of junk. There's a great stall near the market's waterside selling navy/airforce surplus and used shirts, jackets and hoodies to cheaply replenish your wardrobe. It's easy to spend couple of hours wandering around and unlike other Amsterdam markets you can bargain. Open: Mor Sat 10-17. (Map area E6)

Flower Market - Singel

A plethora of flowers and plants are sold here at Amsterdam's only floating flower market. Cut flowers are a good deal, but in recent years the tulip bulb quality has diminished. And nowadays you ca probably get bulbs equally cheap at home. Even if you're not planning on shopping at this ultra-tourist market, it can be interesting to wander though. (Map area D6)

IJ-Hallen – NDSM Werf - T.T. Neveritaweg 15, Amsterdam North

www.ij-hallen.n

Serious bargain hunters arrive early at this giant flea market to score the best deals. But with ove 600 stalls selling everything imaginable, good finds can be made here all day. I once scored a pair c vintage shades for 50 cents! The free ferry that goes here leaves regularly from behind Centraal Sta tion and takes about 10 minutes. It's a fun trip. When you need a break from the crowd at the market grab something to eat at the Noorderlicht (see Cafés), or check out the Skatepark (see Hanging Ou chapter). The market takes place the first weekend of every month – inside in winter, outside in sum mer – from 9-16:30. Admission is €2.50.

books and magazines

Book lovers will love Amsterdam. Dozens of new and second-hand bookstores sell mainly Englis titles, and browsing for European editions can be rewarding. If you're here in May, be sure t check the Amsterdam Literary Festival (*www.amsterdamliteraryfestival.com*), a multi-day celebra tion showcasing both local and international authors inspired by Amsterdam. It takes place in inte esting venues around town and includes readings, workshops plus parties. Another local literar development is the Britlit series of talks (*www.britlit.info*) by well-known British authors. Thes readings sell out so make advance reservations.

The American Book Center - Spui 12, ☎ 625-5537

www.abc.r

This multi-level store is one of Europe's largest English-language book sources stocking hard-to-fin items as well as best sellers. They also carry a large array of collectable photography books, maga zines, comics, toys and a few shelves of American junk food for pathetic expats craving Butterfinger (guilty as charged). Students get a 10% discount; non-students can buy a discount card valid for on year giving 10% off every purchase, making ABC one of Amsterdam's cheapest bookstores. Folk working here are friendly and will gladly help you find specific books. The American Bookstore als hosts an interesting project called the ABC Treehouse in a small gallery nearby, (Voetboogstraat 11 *www.treehouse.abc.nl)* where bookstore volunteers present author lectures, writers' workshops, an open-mike nights. Bookstore open: Mon-Sat 10-20 (Thurs 'til 21); Sun 11-18:30. (Map area D5)

Waterstone's Booksellers - Kalverstraat 152, ☎ 638-3821

www.waterstones.cor

This august but bustling British bookstore chain has its Amsterdam outlet on the Spui square at th corner of the Kalverstraat. There are four levels stuffed with books of all sorts, from current best seller to the classics, and the store offers frequent readings and authors' talks in a cozy space on the to floor. If they haven't got the book you desire in stock they'll order it for you. Next to the English language newspaper rack inside the front door are always *Amsterdam Times* and other local newspapers. Open: Tues-Sat 10-18 (Thurs 'til 21); Mon-Sun 12:30-18 (Map area: D5,6)

The Book Exchange - Kloveniersburgwal 58, ☎ 626-6266

There's no typical used bookstore mustiness and clutter at The Book Exchange, but a clean, well-organized shop with a wide book selection. They have a big travel section with both guides and literature, and there's a German and French section, too. If you have books to sell they pay some of the fairest prices in town. Open: Mon-Sat 10-18; Sun 11:30-16. (Map area E5)

Kok Antiquariaat - Oude Hoogstraat 14-18, ☎ 623 1191

www.nvva.nl/kok

Kok is pleasant used bookstore stuffed with English titles. It's spacious and well organized: English literature is upstairs. Open: Mon-Fri 9:30-18; Sat 9:30-17. (Map area D5)

De Slegte - Kalverstraat 48-52, ☎ 622-5933

www.deslegte.nl

Some good deals can be found at this big store on the Kalverstraat, a long and packed shopping street. It lacks the charm of Kok Antiquariaat (see above), but upstairs you'll find a huge selection of used books, many in English. (A friend of mine found a rare Philip K. Dick novel for €4). Open: Mon 11-18; Tues -Fri 9:30-18 (Thurs 'til 21); Sat 9:30-18; Sun 12-17. (Map area D5)

The English Bookshop - Lauriergracht 71, ☎ 626-4230

www.englishbookshop.nl

Thanks to the current owners' hard work this pretty bookstore is finally living up to its literary hangout potential. Book clubs and writers' groups meet here, and there are also regular poetry, prose and book readings. Upstairs there's a select collection of contemporary and classic works. Coffee, tea, scones and other treats are available for you to munch as you read your paperback and gaze the beautiful, lazy Laurier canal. Downstairs they have a fine selection of children's books, and it's a great place to pick up a souvenir for little ones back home. If you're travelling with young children, catch a Friday morning reading for kids in English. Just two short blocks from the Elandsgracht, a charming shopping street. Open: Tues-Sat 11-18 (Thurs 'til 20). (Map area B5)

Evenaar - Singel 348, ☎ 624-6289

http://travel.to.evenaar

This travel bookshop has a fascinating collection of works organized by region, including guides, journals, novels, history and political analysis—many by lesser-known authors. Worth visiting, especially if you're travelling onward from Holland. Open: Mon-Fri 12-18; Sat 11-17. (Map area C5)

Athenaeum Nieuwscentrum - Spui 14, ☎ 624-2972

www.athenaeum.nl

Athenaeum is one of Amsterdam's best newstands with a wide variety of new magazines and international papers. Check the bargain bin for cheap mags – old music magazines sell here for 50 cents to €2. Athenaeum's sister bookstore next door is excellent and carries a fair number of English titles. Open: Mon-Sat 8-20 (Thurs 'til 21); Sun 10-18. (Map area D5)

The Bookshop - Leidsestraat 106, ☎ 624-0002

This shop also has a big inventory of English-language magazines and daily newspapers from exotic, faraway lands like England and America. They're open early if you want to catch up on the news from back home over breakfast. They also sell snacks and postcards. Located right by the Leidseplein. Open: Mon-Fri 7:30-22; Sat-Sun 8:30-22. (Map area B7)

shopping

De Boekenboom - Spuistraat 230

De Boekenboom is like a San Francisco-style beat bookstore in the heart of Amsterdam. There's a well picked used selection of William Burroughs, Henry Miller and Aldous Huxley, to name a just a handful. A big poster of beat granddaddy Burroughs, pistol in hand, guards the front door. Dusty, cool and owned by a passionate collector. Open: Whenever the owner's not off restocking his supply. (Map area C5)

Het Fort Van Sjakoo - Jodenbreestraat 24, ☎ 625-8979
www.sjakoo.nl

Het Fort specializes in "libertarian and radical ideas from the First to the Fifth World and beyond." This volunteer-run shop has an international political book selection, a whole wall of independent music books, fanzines, magazines, plus lots of anarchism and squatting info. They've got cheap new/used records and CDs, mostly punk, noise and hardcore, plus cards, stickers, patches and shirts (*www. sillyscreens.org*). Psychedelic rock and roll fans: The Fort's resident Dead Head works on Mondays—he will gladly play his favorite shows and discuss all things Grateful Dead. Het Fort is open: Mon-Fri 11-18; Sat 11-17. (Map area E6)

would you buy an anarchist book from this man?

Vrolijk - Paleisstraat 135, ☎ 623-5142
www.vrolijk.nu

Vrolijk, located just off Dam Square, advertises itself as "one of the biggest and best-known gay lesbian bookshops in Europe." Along with books they stock DVDs, magazines and postcards. If you're looking for something in particular, the staff is helpful. Open: Mon 11-18; Tues-Fri 10-18 (Thurs 'til 19) Sat 10-17; Sun 13-17. (Map area D5)

Muzikat - St. Antoniesbreestraat 3G, ☎ 320-0386

You'll find this unique little shop specializing in music books on an ugly stretch of road near the Nieuwmarkt. Its shelves are full of biographies, lyrics, photo books, plus band and genre histories. There are also magazines, posters and a couple of crates of vinyl. Who knows, you just might find that Moon Dog biography or Serge Gainsbourg interview you've been looking for. Across the street at number 64 is a cool vinyl-only shop called Record Friend, with over 20,000 new and used records. Muzikat open Tues-Sat 12-18. (Map area E5)

Book Traffic - Leliegracht 50, ☎ 620-4690

Book Traffic has lots of English books and sometimes puts a bargain bin out front. There are a few other used bookshops located on this beautiful canal as well. Open: Mon-Fri 10-18; Sat 11-18; Sun 13-18 (Map area C4)

Intermale - Spuistraat 251, ☎ 625-0009
www.intermale.n

In case you couldn't tell from the name, this is a gay bookstore. It's a nice space with a good selection of books, magazines and movies. You can pick up gay guides to countries all around the world, an out-of-print book of photos by Larry Clark, or Bruce LaBruce's latest DVD. Open: Mon 11-18; Tues-Sa 10-18; (Thurs 'til 21). (Map area C5)

Henk Lee's Comics & Manga Store - Zeedijk 136, ☎ 421-3688
www.comics.n

Located in Amsterdam's tiny Chinatown, Henk's is stuffed full of comics, toys, trading cards and DVDs His specialty is manga—if you can't find a particular edition, check the Japanese-owned Hotel Okura's basement bookshop. (Ferdinand Bolstraat 333; 679-9238). Henk Lee open: Mon-Sat 11-18 (Thurs 'til 21); Sun 12-18. (Map area E4)

Lambiek - Kerkstraat 132, ☎ 626-7543

www.lambiek.net

This is the oldest and most famous comic store in Amsterdam—where Freak Brothers creator Gilbert Sheldon visits when he's in town. Lambiek carries a huge selection of new and used books, both mainstream (though not superhero) and underground, graphic comics, first editions and signed posters. Check out their exhaustively researched on-line "Comiclopedia" containing entries on more than 7,000 artists. Open: Mon-Fri 11-18; Sat 11-17; Sun 13-17. (Map area C7)

Vandal Com-x - Rozengracht 31, ☎ 420-2144

www.vandalcomx.com

Definitely check this place out if you're into action figures: they've got them from floor to ceiling. You can find everything from Radioactive Cornholio to Nightmare Before Christmas to Judge Dread. (Another good place for TV and film toys is Space Oddity. It's just around the corner at Prinsengracht 204.) Vandal also sells trading cards, shirts, and more. The comix are at their other shop a few doors down the street. Open: Tues-Fri 11-18; Sat 11-17; Sun 12-17. (Map area B5)

Cultural - Gasthuismolensteeg 4, ☎ 624-8793

This hole-in-the-wall bookstore has a few shelves of English paperbacks plus piles of old Lifes and other magazines from the 1950s and '60s. You can even find '60s newspapers published by the Black Panther Party or possibly the "Rock & Roll and Dope" 5th Estate articles written back in the day by our illustrious editor. It's not far from Dam Square, so you might pass it while wandering this attractive area. Open: Mon-Sat 11-18. (Map area C5)

Oudemanhuis Boekenmarkt - Oudemanhuispoort

This little book market, situated in a covered alleyway between Oudezijds Achterburgwal and Kloveniersburgwal near the University of Amsterdam, offers used books and magazines in several languages. There are also maps, cards and, occasionally, funny pornographic etchings from centuries past – just a couple of euros each. Midway down the hall is an entrance to a pretty courtyard with benches where you can rest your legs. Open: Mon-Fri 11-16. (Map area E5)

Alibi - Willemsstraat 21, ☎ 625-0676

www.crime.nl/alibi

Crime fiction devotees freak when they visit Alibi. It's wall-to-wall crime, thrillers, suspense, and more crime. There's a huge selection of both new and used English books, and the owner will gladly help you find both popular plus more obscure titles. She can also recommend books by Dutch writers translated into English. Fans of the genre meet every Sunday at 16:00 for an afternoon of "crime and wine" to catch a buzz and stalk others who share their literary interests. Open: Tues-Fri 11-18; Sat 11-17; Sun 12-17. (Map area C3)

records and cds

Many of my favorite record shops have shut their doors and gone on-line, which I find a shame
Nothing is more satisfying than fingering your way through a fat row of records and finding that elu
sive gem – and there are still a few fine local shops satisfying vinyl junkies and import fetishists.

Concerto - Utrechtsestraat 52-60, ☎ 623-5228

www.concerto.n

Attention collectors: Don't miss Concerto, an eclectic superstore selling new and used LPs, CDs
DVDs plus rare releases spanning multiple genres--dance, indie, modern jazz, vintage country, what
ever your ear desires. It comprises several old storefronts, each with their own specialties, along the
busy Utrechtsestraat. Inside Concerto has crowded rooms jammed with merchandise and prices are
decent for used stuff. Open: Mon-Sat 10-18 (Thurs 'til 21); Sun 12-18. (Map area E7)

Distortion Records - Westerstraat 244, ☎ 627-0004

www.distortion.n

This cluttered store advertises "loads of noise, lo-fi, punk rock and indie," but you'll also find jazz, sou
reggae and a cherry picked selection of dance music. Record collectors will love Distortion; the own
ers are multi-genre vinyl-heads ready to share their expertise. Located just down the street from the
Noordermarkt (see Markets, above). Open: Tues-Fri 11-18 (Thurs 'til 21); Sat 10-18. (Map area C3)

Flesch Books & Records - Noorderkerkstraat 16, ☎ 622-8185

www.fleschrecords.com

Flesch is a high-quality collectors' shop run by a guy who lives in a world where turntables still rule
preferably with mono pickups – and you can hear what 50-year-old records really sound like. Folk, clas
sical, Jazz, '60s Beat and Garage are just some of the genres on offer, in editions from incredibly rar
pressings to well-known titles. You can dig around, listen to some records on vintage turntables or cha
with the owner, a person blessed with encyclopedic music knowledge. Racks of old 45s and musi
books also abound. Out front there are a couple of bargain bins and inexpensive bags of locally grow
apples and pears available. Open: Mon 10-16; Thurs/Fri 13-17; Sat 10-18 (Map area C3)

Record Palace - Weteringschans 33, ☎ 622-3904

www.record palace.com

Record Palace has sections for many kinds of music but their jazz collection is unparalleled. They're a bit pricey but bebop enthusiasts can scope illusive vinyl gems. Check out their autographed record cover display on the wall. Across the street from the famous Paradiso concert hall (see Music chapter). Open: Mon-Fri 11-18; Sat 11-17; Sun 12-17. (Map area C7)

Record Mania - Ferdinand Bolstraat 30, ☎ 620-9912

www.recordmania.nl

Although they carry some CDs, vinyl rules at this pretty southside shop, located in the bustling *De Pijp* neighborhood. It's fantastic being surrounded by full racks of LPs and singles just waiting for discovery. They have collectibles (need the first Nazareth? Or perhaps a four EP Cannonball Adderley release on clear vinyl?) and seriously cheap bargain bins. Open: Mon-Sat 12-18. (Map area C8)

Back Beat Records - Egelantiersstraat 19, ☎ 627-1657

www.backbeat.nl

Blues, Afrobeat, R&B, jazz, funk, soul: a slew of records and CDs are all packed into three levels at the glorious Back Beat. It's not cheap, but what a selection! Located in the Jordaan. Open: Mon-Fri 11-18; Sat 10-17. (Map area C4)

Independent Outlet - Vijzelstraat 77, ☎ 421-2096

www.outlet.nl

IO is punk and hardcore central, with loads of vinyl (of course), CDs and band tee-shirts. This is the source for a Black Flag tee, an original D.R.I. record or an Agent Orange "Living in Darkness" reprint (see Misc, this chapter). Open: Sun-Mon 13-18; Tues-Sat 11-18 (Thurs 'til 21). (Map area D7)

Second Life Music - Prinsengracht 366, ☎ 064-542-6344

www.secondlifemusic.nl

Second Life has an excellent collection of reasonably priced vintage music. They sell mainly vinyl, though a few CDs are also available. There is a nice selection of bargain bins to peruse, or check the old-school turntables piled in the back. Open: Tues-Sun 13-18. (Map area B6)

Velvet Music - Rozengracht 40, ☎ 422-8777

www.velvetmusic.nl

Velvet Music has several stores nationwide. The Amsterdam location does a bustling business buying and selling new and used LPs and CDs. My friend snagged a really hot Fela Kuti record here for a good price in the used vinyl bins. There's also a small box in the back which occasionally has old issues of *Mojo* and other music magazines for €1 to €2.50. Open: Mon 12-18; Tues-Sat 10-18 (Thurs 'til 21). (Map area B4)

Rush Hour Records - Spuistraat 98, ☎ 427-4505

www.rushhour.nl

Rush Hour is popular with DJs who come to hear what's new and hot. The owners have their own label and distribute at least a couple of dozen others. There are also bins full of used records: funk, soul, African, dub and other genres with a dance beat. They also sell a small selection of books, shirts, slip-mats and record bags. Other shops selling dance music in the neighborhood include: Killa Cutz at Nieuwe Nieuwstraat 19; InDeep'n Dance at Rozengracht 60; Groove Connection at St. Nicolaasstraat 50. Rush Hour is located right next door to Female and Partners (see Sex chapter). Open: Mon 13-19; Tues-Sat 11-19 (Thurs 'til 21); Sun 13-18. (Map area C5)

used clothing stores

In Amsterdam, like most hip cities, when the term "vintage" took off, the price of second-hand clothing skyrocketed. Nevertheless, here are a few shops where you might still find decent deals.

Noordermarkt - Noordermarkt

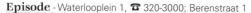

There's literally tons of used clothing at this fabulous market (see above). Go early for the bargains. Open: Mon only, 9-14. (Map area C3)

Episode - Waterlooplein 1, ☎ 320-3000; Berenstraat 1

Both of these shops have vast clothing and accessory selections, many from '70s and '80s North America. Episode is constantly renewing its hand picked supply much loved by retro chic locals and tourists. One store is located at a corner of the Waterlooplein flea market (there's lots of used clothing there, too - see Markets, above). The other is in the quaint shopping mecca called the 9 Streets (*9 Straatjes*.) Open: Mon-Sat 10-18. (Map area E6)

Zipper - Nieuwe Hoogstraat 10, ☎ 627-0353

Vintage clothing fans swamp this split-level shop; the owners know what style-conscious shoppers look for and stock accordingly. They also have another store, in the 9 Streets, at Huidenstraat 7. Open Mon 13-18; Tues-Sat 11-18; Sun 13-17. (Map area D5)

Wini - Haarlemmerstraat 29 - ☎ 427-9393

Wini is a popular shop just a few minutes walk from Centraal Station. It's packed full of retro fashion, including plenty of seasonal accessories, in case you didn't pack right for the weather. Open: Mon 11-18; Tues-Sat 10:30-18 (Thurs 'til 20). (Map Area D3)

Vind It - Tweede Egelantiersdwaarsstraat 7, ☎ 063-839-6106

www.vinditvintage.nl

Vind it means "find it" in Dutch. Finding this tiny shop located in the picturesque *Jordaan* neighborhood can be a challenge, but a worthwhile one. Fans of vintage clothing, especially in a rockabilly and ska-type vein, will enjoy this place. A few racks of clothes are there for perusing, along with a CD wall full of mostly unknown local bands. Grab a CD, support local talent and brag to your friends back home about the hip new Dutch band you dig. The owners are a friendly couple that throw parties and know a great deal about the Amsterdam music scene. Open: Tues-Thurs 12-18; Fri-Sat 11-18. (Map Area C4)

tattoos and piercing

Many fine tattoo artists call Amsterdam home, so if you plan getting inked on your travels check out one of the reputable places below, or search online for shops specializing in specific styles.

Tattoo Peter - Nieuwebrugsteeg 28, ☎ 626-6372

www.tattoopeter.nl

Tattoo Peter, one of the world's oldest skin art shops, is located on the edge of the Red Light District - one of Amsterdam's oldest historic areas. Sailors used to line up to get tattooed here and you can still almost smell the blood and ink. Check out Peter's website for some classic old pics. The studio enjoys an international reputation for its first-rate, quality artists. Open: Daily 12-20. (Map area E4)

House of Tattoos - Haarlemmerdijk 130c, ☎ 330-9046

www.houseoftattoos.nl

Sjap, who opened this studio, used to work at Tattoo Peter (see above). He specializes in one-of-a-kind pieces. Renowned artists work here and the environment is relaxed. This place gets busy, so an appointment is always a good idea--you'll be guaranteed to get needled--but walk-ins are also welcome. Open: Mon-Sat 11-18; Sun 13-18. (Map area C2)

Derma Donna - Kloveniersburgwal 34, ☎ 773-6614

www.dermadonna.com

This relaxed little tattoo shop, owned by an artist who specializes in unique custom work, is set in a beautiful old canal house near the Nieuwmarkt. Cool jazz was playing the last time I visited as Rosana colored a tattoo in progress vibrant blue. Some striking examples of her work are on the wall, and she offers a personal consultation about your idea before starting to ink you. She once tattooed Thai food – including shrimps, lime wedges and chili peppers – on a cuisine-obsessed customer! Check out her website for examples of her work. She's world-renowned and books out at least two months in advance, so it's wise to make an appointment. If you visit Bermuda, check out her new shop—this tattoo entrepeneur is going global. Derma Donna also has rotating guest tattoo artists who take walk-ins. Open: Daily 12-19 (Map area D5)

Derma Donna

Dare 2 Wear - Buiten Oranjestraat 15, ☎ 686-8679

www.dare2wear.nl

For the highest-quality piercings in Amsterdam, look no further than this sweet little studio just off the Haarlemmerdijk. It's a clean, professional shop, with a restful atmosphere. Most of the piercers are women, and they're more than happy to talk to you about the procedure and what pain (if any) is involved. They also have one of the largest collections of ethnic jewellery in Europe, including beautiful pieces made of stone, wood, horn and bone. Sample prices for a piercing, including jewellery: €25 for an ear, €45 for one nipple (€80 for two), €50 for a tongue, and €60-€70 for genitals. It's €5 extra if you want a bar instead of a ring. There are lots of other options, of course. Have fun! Open: Sun 13-18; Mon 13-19; Tues-Sat 12-19. (Map area C2)

Classic Ink & Mods - Spaarpotsteeg 2, ☎ 753-9652

www.classicinkandmods.com

This tattoo/piercing parlor was started by Sharon, the woman who owns Dare 2 Wear. You'll find her multi-level shop tucked into a narrow alley and you can see people getting inked through a panoramic window at the entrance. The front room boasts some fantastic paintings on its walls, from sexy ink-covered pinups to Bali demons. A relaxed vibe emanates here from the friendly staff and the team of highly respected female piercers, including the master herself, who work on the second level. The top story houses another tattooing space, a light-colored wooden interior with beautiful Japanese prints. They also do body modification, splitting, implants – anything your tender flesh desires. Open: Mon-Sun 12-19; Thur 12-21. (Map area C, D 5)

hair

If you're having a bad hair day everyday—time to clean up that mop! Just because you're travelling doesn't mean you can't rock a new 'do. Amsterdam has literally hundreds of hair salons, cheap and pricey. Check out Cut the Crap (Haarlemerplein 9, map area C2) or Barrio (Eerste Anjelierdwarstraat 1, map area C4) for hip cuts. Below are a couple of more options.

Salon Haar & Gezondheid - Amstel 186, ☎ 427-2477

www.salonhaarengezondheid.nl

This place is a unique hair-coloring salon using exclusively chemical free vegetable-based dyes. Choose from 40 different colors. Open: Tues-Fri 10-18; Sat 9:30-17. (Map area D6)

Free Haircuts - Voormalige Stadstimmertuinen 1, ☎ 530-7230

You can get a free haircut from a grateful student at this academy. There are always supervisors nearby so you shouldn't come out looking like Crusty the Clown, but it might take a while. Call for an appointment. (Map area F7). There's another hair school at Weteringschans 167 (626-3430) that has a pretty good rep and cheap prices. You don't need to call in advance. (Map area D8)

chocolate

Pompadour - Huidenstraat 12, ☎ 623-9554; Kerkstraat 158, ☎ 330-0981

Cocoa lovers have been making pilgrimages to this chocolate mecca for over 40 years. There are cakes, cookies and croissants to choose from, as well as almost 50 different bonbons. The staff exhibits remarkable patience going over what's what for the umpteenth time, but it's easy to fill up a box with chocolate treats – or just buy one or two for a taste. In the back there's an old-fashioned tearoom where you can linger over a hot drink and something sweet. They have a newer, trendier shop in the Kerkstraat, too. Open: Mon-Fri 9-18; Sat 9-17. (Map Area C5)

Puccini Bomboni - Staalstraat 17, ☎ 626-5474; Singel 184, ☎ 427-8341

www.puccinibomboni.com

Puccini's luxurious bonbons are created in house at this small but swanky boutique near the Waterlooplein market. Their menu includes strange flavors like black pepper, chili and lemongrass--their gin variety is a beautifully bizarre mouthful of happiness. Chocolates are sold by weight; a small box costs about €10, or by the piece. Puccini also has a shop on the Singel across the street from the Grey Area (see Coffeeshops). Staalstraat Open: Sun-Mon 12-18; Tues-Sat 9-18. (Map area D6)

Unlimited Delicious - Haarlemmerstraat 122, ☎ 622-4829

www.unlimiteddelicious.nl

Adventurous chocolate fans enjoy exploring the many unconventional flavor combinations like "tomato balsamic pimento" offered here, and tamer tastebuds can go for more traditional bonbons. They also sell homemade ice cream and some amazing-looking cakes and tarts, which you can enjoy with an espresso. Open: Mon-Fri 9-18; Sat 9-17. (Map area D3)

Leonidas Bon Bons - Schiphol Airport, arrivals level, ☎ 653-5077

www.leonidas.com

If you need a couple of last minute gifts, Belgian chocolate, even from a big corporation like Leonidas, is a delicious option. Their assorted boxes make tasty presents, and the airport branch prices are equal to city prices. Grab some for yourself, too—enjoy some Belgian love instead of crappy airplane food. Open: Daily 7-22.

smart shops

good ole 'shrooms

Some years ago, the Dutch Ministry of Health decided hallucinogenic mushrooms are not hazardous when used responsibly. Dried and fresh mushrooms were sold openly in specialized "smart shops," selling hallucinogenic wares. Due to EU and US pressure the Dutch government ended its tolerance and banned all mushrooms, even fresh ones. Smart shops had 'shroom clearance sales to get rid of their stock before the ban took place. But check this: psychedelic truffles, known locally as "philosopher stones" are still available. Truffles and mushrooms are not in the same family...so the ban doesn't apply. Other psychoactive plants and cacti are also available, as well as herbal stimulants, relaxants, aphrodisiacs and natural mixtures to turn you on or lay you down. Here are a few reputable shops.

Kokopelli - Warmoesstraat 12, ☎ 421-7000

www.kokopelli.nl

Kokopelli is one of Amsterdam's hippest smart shops. The space is beautiful, with a very mellow area at the back to chill out, surf the net, listen to DJs and enjoy the stunning water view. The staff is tourist-friendly, so feel free to ask for info on herbal ecstasy, smart drugs, or any other products on offer. They also have collectible toys and naughty knic-knacs. Located very close to Centraal Station. Open: Daily 11-22. (Map area E4)

Kokopelli

HERBS OF THE GODS

Azarius - Kerkstraat 119, ☎ 489-7914

www.azarius.net

Amsterdam's premier vaporizer boutique, Azarius has upwards of 30 models on display from old school glass to pocket sized battery-powered hitters. The shop is involved in the first Dutch university sponsored medicinal vapor study —that's how dedicated they are to the cause! They also carry a wide array of herbal stimulants, mind relaxers, psychedelic truffles, vitamin supplements and natural energizers. Any questions you may have will be patiently answered by the in shop expert, who is ultra cool and relaxed. Azarius is also one of the top mail order smart shops currently online. Open: Tues-Thurs 12-18, Fri-Sat 12-21 (Map area C7)

The Botanic Herbalist - Nieuwe Herengracht 58, ☎ 470-0889

www.pollinator.nl

The Botanic Herbalist is Amsterdam's most renowned psychoactive plant center. Many varieties are sold, like peyote and the rare Salvia (both leaves and extract)--employees at this laid-back shop know all the plants and their uses. There are also books on all things psychedelic and hemp products from companies like Euro-American Marketing (*www.hemp-amsterdam.com*). They share the space with the Pollinator Company (see Grow Shops, Cannabis chapter) Open: Mon 12-19; Tues-Fri 11-19; Sat 12-19. (Map area E6)

miscellaneous

Independent Outlet - Vijzelstraat 77, ☎ 421-2096

www.outlet.nl

IO is a fantastic, unique store selling punk and hardcore records, band teeshirts, skateboards, sneakers, DIY fanzines, lunch boxes and more. The stylin' clothes here are decently priced for Northern Europe. This is also the place for skate event info and punk/hardcore gig flyers. If you're lucky, you might catch one of their legendary in-store shows: ask at the counter. Open: Mon 13-18; Tues-Sat 11-18 (Thurs 'til 21); Sun 13-18. (Map area D7)

Aboriginal Art and Instruments - Paleisstraat 137, ☎ 423-1333

www.aboriginalart.nl

This is Europe's premier didgeridoo shop and Aboriginal art gallery. The owner travels to the Australian outback and hand picks the most unique and high quality instruments. Some of the world's most famous players have performed using instruments from this shop. If you already have a didgeridoo, stop by for info about jam sessions and workshops. Open: Tues-Sat 12-18; Sun 14-18. (Map area D5)

Vega-Life – Singel 110

www.vega-life.nl

Vega-Life is a little paradise for vegetarian and vegan shoppers interested in sweatshop-free clothing, shoes and accessories. They also stock organic wine, anarchy-emblazoned baby clothes, vegetarian dog food and vegan vitamin supplements. Opened by a member of Holland's political group "Party for Animals," Vega-Life is pro-active in bringing nature and commerce together. Open Tues-Fri 10-18; Sat 10-17 (Map area: C,D4)

The Fair Trade Shop - Heiligeweg 45, ☎ 625-2245

Crafts, clothes and jewellery from developing countries are sold here, as well as fair-trade coffee, tea, chocolate, nuts and wine. They have plenty of unusual planet-conscientious gift items. Open: Mon 13-18; Tues Fri 10 -18 (Thurs 'til 21), Sat 10-17:30; Sun 12-17. (Map area D6)

shopping

China Town Liquor Store - Geldersekade 94-96, ☎ 624-5229

Located in a sleazy strip of Amsterdam's China Town, this well stocked liquor store has an immense stock and some good bargains. A couple of doors down is a cheap Chinese supermarket, Wah Nam Hong. There's a swankier liquor store in the basement of the Albert Heijn on Nieuwezijds Voorburgwal, and one in the Dirk van den Broek at the Heinekenplein (see Supermarkets, Food chapter) that are open later. The China Town Liquor Store: Open: Mon-Sat 9-18. (Map area E4)

Dodo - 1e Van Der Helstraat 21, ☎ 671-2151

There are some gems among all the old clothes, books, toys, and records at this grungy, low price second-hand shop, but you'll have to dig to get lucky – most things are crap. One friend of mine found an excellent '70s Telly Sevalas country record here, with songs about driving trucks and popping pills. If you're wandering though the busy streets off of the Albert Cuyp Market, then this place is worth a look, but don't go out of your way. For a bigger thrift store, check out De Lokatie (Beijersweg 12) in the east end of the city, or the Juttersdok (below). Dodo: Open: Mon 13-18; Tues-Fri 10-18; Sat 10-17.

Juttersdok - Zeeburgerpad 90; Postjeskade 23

www.juttersdok.n

These local shops are similar to authentic American-style thrift stores-- filled with clothes, records books, videos, furniture, appliances and everything else. Prices are cheap and profits go to a variety of good causes. If you're seriously into bargain hunting these are fun places to poke around. Zeeburgerpad is in the east, past the IJ Brewery (see Bars). Postjeskade is in the west, near Rembrandtpark Open: Mon 13-17:30; Tues-Fri 9:30-17:30; Sat 9:30-17. (Map area J6)

Donalds E Jongelans - Noorderkerkstraat 18, ☎ 624-6888

Ever walked into an old-style corner store and find a stylish pair of sunglasses in a dusty display case? That's what this store feels like, except it's not dusty. They have a fantastic selection of old (but not used) sunglasses and frames at reasonable prices. The owner once repaired my broken shades for free–that's cool, and not common in this city. It's right behind the Noorderkerk, (see Markets, above). Open: Mon-Sat 11-18. (Map area C3)

De Witte Tandenwinkel - Runstraat 5, ☎ 623-3443

www.dewittetandenwinkel.nl

This store has a huge front window displaying part of the world's largest toothbrush collection—all shapes, sizes and styles. They make unusual gifts, and don't weigh much – a bonus when you're travelling. You'll find De Witte Tandenwinkel in the Nine Streets neighborhood. Open: Mon 13-18; Tues-Fri 10-18; Sat 10-17. (Map area C5)

Studio Spui - Spui 4, ☎ 623-6926

www.studiospui.com

Old school photography fans still using film can check this camera shop for special deals on rolls near expiration. The studio also stocks loads of accessories for digital cameras. Open: Mon 10:30-18; Tues-Fri 9:30-18 (Thurs 'til 21); Sat 10-17:30. (Map area D5)

free postcards

If you don't care whether Amsterdam is pictured on the cards you send home, look for the Boomerang free postcard racks in movie theatre lobbies, cafés and bars all over town. One of my past favorites is a painting of Jesus with the caption: "Jesus is coming...look busy!"

Hanging Out

This chapter is for people who enjoy wandering the streets, peeping the local population, listening to music in the park--and those of you who are broke. During warmer months Amsterdam's streets and parks come alive; you don't need a lot of money to find entertainment. I've also included some suggestions for when it's rainy or cold.

parks

Amsterdam is a green city boasting several beautiful parks used throughout the year, but particularly in the summer months when the famous multi-hued, lingering sunsets last 'till late. Picnics are very popular in Holland – you can invite all your friends at once, instead of the small number that could fit in the typically tiny apartments here. After dark, however, it's best not to hang out in any of these parks alone.

Vondelpark

www.vondelpark.org

When the weather is warm this is Amsterdam's most happening place, especially on Sundays. Inline skaters, joggers and bicycles cruise the smooth pavement while crowds of people stroll the park enjoying the sunshine and the eclectic atmosphere. Little paths lead through leafy woods and out into fields where active people kick balls, throw Frisbees, do yoga or generally get sweaty. Old men fish in quiet ponds only minutes away from a band shell with live music. There's an impressive fragrant rose garden, a Picasso sculpture and a meadow with cows, goats and llamas. Bright green parrots sit in the trees and people recline half-naked on the grass, reading, picnicking, drinking beer, smoking joints, playing chess and sleeping. Trams: 1, 2, 5. (Map area A8)

Amsterdamse Bos (Woods)

www.amsterdamsebos.amsterdam.nl

It's a mini mission finding your way to this humungous park, but it's Amsterdam's largest green patch and a wanderer's paradise. Winding bike and hiking paths, a farmhouse pancake restaurant (see Kids) a fresh water lake, an open-air theater, a Japanese garden, tree top adventures, a gay cruising zone, terrace cafés, outdoor parties—the Bos is happening in the summer. There's a big field to lie back and watch jets from nearby Schiphol airport fly right over you. Fans of psychedelics love to trip here. You can rent bikes, canoes, kayaks and boats if walking gets boring. Free maps and information are available from the visitors' center (on Bosbaanweg 5; 545-6100; open daily from 12 to 17:00). Buses: 170, 172 from Centraal Station.

Oosterpark (East Park)

Lots of ducks and toddlers waddle around this splendid park. It's also full of people simply strolling along the water's edge or playing soccer in the big field. A variety of festivals and parties are held here, including the Oosterpark Festival in the first week of May and the fantastic Roots Festival in June (see Music chapter). During past Holland Festivals (also in June; *www.hollandfestival.nl*) live opera was broadcasted via giant screens to crowds of picnickers. Near the gazebo is a "speaker's corner" where on Sunday afternoons anyone can step up and start blabbing. And, since drums of any kind were banned in Vondelpark, Oosterpark draws percussionists galore. It's right by the Dappermarkt (see Markets, Shopping chapter), and the Tropenmuseum (see Museums chapter). Trams 3, 7, 9. (Map area G8)

Sarphatipark

This pretty little park in *De Pijp* is close to the Albert Cuyp Market (see Markets, Shopping chapter) plus Katsu and YoYo (see Coffeeshops, Cannabis chapter). You can grab a sack and some cheap market eats then come here to puff and stuff. Trams: 16, 24, 25.

Westerpark - (West Park)

A huge, open lawn full of sunning, frisbee tossing, football kicking folks bustles during the summer. There's something for everyone here: tapas style eats and lounging at the Westergasterras, Italian coffee at the Espresso Fabriek, the hip weekend music venue Pacific Parc (see Music chapter), a kiddie wading pool, a pond full of ducks and geese plus plenty of trails to explore. In winter the aquaduct-like pond turns into an ice skating rink when the weather dips below freezing. Many famous artists like Radiohead, Björk and Leonard Cohen have given summer concerts on the big lawn. (Ticketless visitors can relax on the upper lawn with a beer or a joint and hear the tunes for free.) Located just west of the Centrum, 5 minutes past Haarlemmerpoort.

Wertheimpark

This petite park, Napoleon's gift to Amsterdam, sits adjacent to a peaceful canal just a couple of blocks from the Waterlooplein flea market (see Markets, Shopping chapter). Sitting under the large waterside trees is a great way to mellow out, cool your heels and catch your breath after battling the market crowds. It's also directly across the street from the Botanical Gardens (see Museums chapter). Tram: 9. (Map area F6)

public squares

Begijnhof

www.begijnhofamsterdam.nl

The Begijnhof is a famous old courtyard in Amsterdam's historic center. Look for an entrance behind the Amsterdam Museum on the Gedempte Begijnensloot just above the Spui. Inside, there's a plaque describing architectural history of churches and buildings surrounding the idyllic garden-filled courtyard. Amsterdam's oldest house—built in 1425—is also located here. Visiting hours are limited because busloads of loud tourists disturb the elderly residents, but it's still open daily from 8 to 13:00. (Map area C6).

Leidseplein

At the far end of this popular square several bronze lizard sculptures lie in flower-dotted grass. Across the street, carved high up on mach Roman marble pillars, is that age-old proverb: *Homo Sapiens Non Urinat In Ventum*, which is Latin for "don't piss in the wind." If the weather is good street performers are busy in the squares's main section, by the tram stops. Break dancers, unicyclists, fire eaters, magicians and jugglers entertain crowds here—sometimes lining up, waiting for their chance to make some dough. In the wintertime there's an ice-skating rink, too. Trams: 1, 2, 5, 7, 10. (Map area 7B)

Museumplein

Some of Holland's most famous museums are situated around this giant square. Major renovations have generated all sorts of problems on the Museumplein, but except for the underground parking garages, it's pretty nice. There's a new extra-wide mini-ramp with multiple transitions for skaters, bladers or BMXers and the basketball courts are back if you want to shoot hoops. Sometimes in winter there's an ice-skating rink, with skate rental available. Trams: 2, 3, 5. (Map area C8)

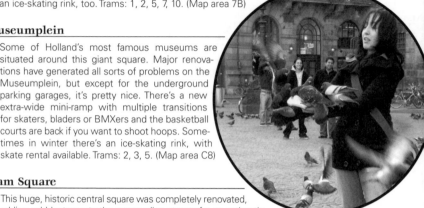

Dam Square

This huge, historic central square was completely renovated, adding cobblestones to the surrounding streets for an authentic antique-city simulation. It's quiet in the winter, but buzzing daily in the summer. Unfortunately, a lot of pickpockets and other sleazy creeps like to hang here. Keep your eye open and don't buy drugs from any of the scummy dealers: you'll definitely get ripped off. (Map area D4)

Nieuwmarkt

Nieuwmarkt (New Market) is an alluring Amsterdam square located at the edge of the Red Light District and China Town. There's a stunning 15th-century castle-like building smack dab in the middle. It used to be a weigh station, and upstairs in one of the turrets were autopsy and surgery theaters where criminal corpses had their insides diagrammed. Now it just houses a posh, busy café. Small shops, bars and restaurants surround the entire square. The numerous outdoor terraces here are especially lively on sunny days and become popular drinking spots at night. There's an organic market on Saturdays (see Markets, Shopping chapter). And on New Year's Eve, thousands of people gather here to party and set off an intense mega fire-works display. (Map area E5)

libraries

Public Library - Oosterdokskade 143, ☎ 523-0900

www.oba.

This seven-story monster library is Europe's largest. Only members can borrow books, but there are lots of interesting happenings and exhibitions here, and it can be great on a rainy day. In case you need a little lubrication, there's a fully stocked bar to the right once you get inside. Between the ground and first floors is an international newspaper and magazine reading room where worldwide print media is delivered daily. There's a café where you can get a coffee and croissant for about €3.50 and catch up on current events where you're from – nice to have if you've been traveling a while. A great view of the train tracks is on one side of the room and the giant atrium-like library on the other. Further up the escalator are the various sections: On the music floor, live concerts and performances from classical quartets to jazz pianists to Hawaiian guitar bands take place, and there's a reading plaza here named after famous artist-composer-rock & roll junkie Herman Brood that displays several of his paintings. The OBA also has free internet access and music-listening facilities for auditing the thousands of CDs in stock. On the top level is a La Place restaurant with its fresh, made-to-order cafeteria feel and extensive menu selection – everything from multi-fruit smoothies to noodle dishes to apple pie. A terrace with a stunning city view awaits you. If you're traveling with kids, they have a full children's section downstairs with individual little open-roofed houses where youngsters may read, surf the internet, and even climb around in different spaces like the two-level "Dream House." (Map area: E4)

Pintohuis Library - Sint Antoniesbreestraat 69, ☎ 624-3184

During the early 1970s this 17th-century house was nearly demolished to widen the street. Fortunately, activists who squatted the building saved it. After a complete restoration it was re-opened as a library. Petite rooms, old wooden furniture and high fresco-covered ceilings make Pintohuis a peaceful place for reading or pondering. Upstairs they host art exhibitions – *Erotic Paintings* was the last one I checked. Open: Mon-Wed 14-20; Fri 14-17; Sat 11-16. (Map area E5)

internet cafés

The Amsterdam internet café boom is over, but many cafés and coffeeshops have computers for surfing or checking email. Free WiFi also abounds.

The Mad Processor - Kinkerstraat 11-13, ☎ 612-1818

www.madprocessor.com

One of the first cool internet cafés, The Mad Processor is now the last cool internet café—the WiFi/Smartphone revolution caused other locales to permanently close their doors. The two front rooms of this comfortable joint are set up for surfing and checking e-mail. Printers and scanners are available (scanning is free if you do it yourself), plus you can upload pics from your camera and burn them for just the price of a disc (€1). Internet use costs 50 cents for 10 minutes, but you can buy three hours pre-paid for €7.50, or 5 hours for €10. The popular back room is set up for gaming, both face-to-face and on-line, and you can smoke cannabis while you play. There's not much available here food and beverage wise, but a candy-vending machine and caffeinated drinks are available to fuel your killing frenzies. Open: Daily 12-2. (Map area A6)

free concerts

Het Concertgebouw - Concertgebouwplein 2, ☎ 671-8345

www.concertgebouw.nl

Every Wednesday at 12:30 this famous classical concert hall, world-renowned for its acoustics, throws open its doors to the proletariat for a free half-hour performance. These concerts are extremely popular, so whether it's in the main hall (2000 seats) or the smaller one (500 seats), get there early. Closed in the summer.

Het Concertgebuow

Club 3VOOR12 - Desmet Studios - Plantage Middenlaan 4a, ☎ 671-2222
http://3voor12.vpro.nl/3voor12

I was upset when the Desmet movie theater – where I saw Faster Pussycat Kill Kill on the big screen – closed down, but cultural events like the taping of the live radio show, Club 3VOOR12 keep the creative spirit at this classic space alive. Every Wednesday from 10 to 1:00 bands and solo performers play short sets in front of a studio audience. Both local and international artists play all types of music, from folk to live techno. Sometimes a band doing a show at the Melkweg or Paradiso will do a set here. Tickets are free, but you have to e-mail or call to reserve. There are no concerts in the summer. (Map area F6)

Het Bethaniënklooster - Barndesteeg 6B, ☎ 625-0078
www.bethanienklooster.n

While strolling this shadowy alley in the Red Light District, it's easy to miss the low-key entrance to a remarkable centuries-old cloister. But inside, the building has been beautifully restored and maintained and houses a concert hall. Students from the Amsterdam Conservatory play a lunchtime rehearsal concert every Friday at 12:30 under a row of chandeliers hanging from an archaic, wood-beamed ceiling. There's no charge, but a hat is passed around at the end. There's also a regular program featuring chamber music and, twice a month, "Jazz at the Monastery." Closed in summer. (Map area 4E)

snowboarding and skateboarding

Much of Holland is below sea level, so you probably wouldn't expect to ski or snowboard here. But if you need a fix, Snow Planet (Heuvelweg 6, 025-554-5848; *www.snowplanet.nl*) has two indoor slopes and a small terrain park complete with hits and obstacles for €19 an hour. Equipment rental is €7.50. It's out of town: To get there, take the Metro to Sloterdijk station and catch bus 82 (toward Ijmuiden). Open: Daily 9-23 (Sept-Apr); shorter hours in summer.

As for skateboarding, your first stop should be Skatepark Everland at NDSM Werf (T.T. Neveritaweg 064-170-0767; *www.skateparkamsterdam.nl*). (See Live Venues, Music chapter.) Skaters designed the entire park, which includes a half-pipe, a mini-ramp pool and obstacles galore. The space is actually suspended from the roof of the massive NDSM building – an amazing sight. The easiest way to get there is to take the ferry behind Centraal Station to NDSM. It leaves every 30 minutes at a quarter past and a quarter to the hour. Then it's just a few minutes walk to the skatepark. Look for lots of graffiti and the black-and-yellow doors at the entrance. Open: Tues-Fri 15-22; Sat-Sun 12-20

Here are a few outdoor skate spots around town:

Skatescape - This figure-eight-shaped pool on the Eerste Marnixplantsoen is a hot spot with skaters, bladers and BMXers. No vert.

Flevopark - A giant half-pipe: east of the park, under the highway bridge. Scary metal ramp with lots of vert.

Museumplein - Two wide mini-ramps connected, spine in the middle, various heights.

Oosterpark - A small street course with some nice obstacles (see Parks, above).

Java Island - Similar to Oosterpark but nicer – and easier on your board.

Olympiaplein - A long quarter, some pyramids and other ramps.

Orteliuspad - A small park with a cement quarter-pipe, hip, spine, and some street obstacles.

For more detailed advice and info on skateboarding in Amsterdam, stop in at Independent Outlet (see Shopping chapter), or Reprezent (Haarlemmerstraat 80; 528-5540): they know what's up.

disc golf

Attention chain heads! Amsterdam now boasts the longest 18-basket par course in the Netherlands, situated in a serene west side park. It's mostly flat terrain, but has a plethora of features: cement tees, water hazards, tight trees, hook shots, mandatories and sometimes painful out of bounds –stinging nettle grows in abundance! Frequent wind and rain make this course even more challenging. A round is free but losing discs in the mucky water or gnarly nettle is the norm here. And watch out for elderly folks strolling the park. It's not a good move to nail a Dutch senior citizen in the head (I've seen it happen) so pay attention–no matter how high you may be.

Hole 10 is a tight line through trees full of nesting Herons. These huge birds make a hell of a racket and look like pterodactyls as they fly overhead.

Discs are available at Sloterbad, an indoor pool complex located next to Sloterpark, where the course is. There's no pro shop, you have to walk upstairs to the pool's reception and ask to see what discs they have. Although sponsored by Discraft, there's a pretty limited selection.

Joe's Vlieger Winkel (Nieuwe Hoogstraat 3) has recently starting selling discs and has a broader selection, but the plastic here is high priced. Best bet is to bring your own bag when visiting Amsterdam!

Directions: Take tram 14 to the end of the line, walk south on President Allendelaan towards the Sloterbad, just after the pool, the park begins. The first tee is in some trees, next to the fence separating Sloterbad and Sloterpark, near the parks entrance, where you'll also find a full map posted. Holes are marked at every tee, with OBs, distance, par and path to the next hole. Intrepid types with bikes can peddle here in about 30-40 minutes from the city center. Find Slotermeer (a Westside lake) on a map that includes the entire city—Sloterpark runs along the lakes west shore.

kite flying and juggling

Because it's flat and windy, Holland is a great country for kite flying, especially at the beach. Wanna buy something to fly? Check Joe's Vliegerwinkel. (Nieuwe Hoogstraat 3; 625-0139; www.joesvliegerwinkel.nl). They sell kites, discs and footbags too. (Map area E5)

For juggling props, from balls and clubs to diabolos and torches, plus info about national and international juggling events, stop by The Juggle Store (Staalstraat 3; 420-1980; www.juggle-store.com). They've also got an awesome selection of yo-yos. Open: Tues-Sat 12-17. (Map area D6)

tower climbing and view gazing

Great views! Good exercise! Get off your ass!

Westerkerkstoren - Westermarkt

The highest. Open: Apr-Sept: Daily 11-15; €5. (Map area C4)

www.westerkerk.nl

Zuiderkerkstoren - Zuiderkerk

The oldest. Open: Jun-Sept: Wed-Sat 14-16 (on the hour); €3. (Map area E5)

Great views! No exercise! Sit on your ass!

Kalvertoren - Singel 457

Café on top of a shopping center. Open: Daily 10-18:30. (Map area D6).

Metz & Co. - Leidsestraat 34

Café on top of a department store. Open: Mon 11-18; Tues-Sat 9:30-18 (Thurs 'til 21); Sun 12-17 (Map area C6)

Openbare Bibliotheek Amsterdam - Oosterdokskade 143

A restaurant/café occupies the top floor of Europe's largest library (see Libraries, this chapter) with panoramic city view.

NeMo - Oosterdok 2

If it's not too windy, the science museum's big deck is a nice place to hang for a bit and peak the lovely old boats in the surrounding docks. Just climb the big steps out front and remember to take some munchies. In the summer they have a bar and loungey beanbag chairs but charge admission (which includes a drink). Sometimes there are DJs, too. Open: Daily 10-17 ('til 21:00 in July and August). (Map area F3)

cloud gazing

Holland is as flat as its proverbial pancakes and clouds – from wispy to fat and fluffy – can move through the sky fast as time-lapse film. On a warm day you can lay on your back in one of Amsterdam's parks (Westerpark's big, open lawn, for instance) and space out on the sky.

Just north of Amsterdam you'll find the real authentic windmill-dotted countryside for which Holland is famous. This landscape was inspirational for many great Dutch painters and

erfect spot to cloud gaze. If you rent a bike, the shop will have detailed maps and routes to 15th-entury villages like Durgerdam, where the picturesque sky meets the famous Dutch inland sea.

saunas and massage therapy

auna Fenomeen - 1e Schinkelstraat 14, ☎ 671-6780

www.saunafenomeen.nl

Despite being in a squat – now legalized – this health club is clean, modern, and well equipped. People of all ages, shapes and sizes come here. Give your name when you enter, grab a towel and get a locker key from the reception. There's a changing room on the left with instructions and rules in both English and Dutch. Then get naked, have a shower and try out the big sauna or the Turkish steam bath. Fenomeen also has a café serving fresh fruit, sandwiches, juices and teas-- a relaxing place to unwind and read the paper or just listen to music and veg. Massages, tranquillity tanks and tanning beds are available at extra charges. Monday is for women only, and the rest of the week is mixed. It's located just past the far end of Vondelpark. Since it's a bit out of the center, you might want to consider combining a visit here with dinner at MKZ (see Restaurants, Food chapter) or an event at OCCII (see Live Venues, Music chapter). Open: daily 13-23. Closed in August.

auna Deco - Herengracht 115, ☎ 623-8215

www.saunadeco.nl

Want something a bit more luxurious? Art Deco fans should try out this sauna. Much of the interior-- lamps, railings, staircases--was rescued and restored from a 1920s Parisian department store during a renovation. They have two sauna rooms, a steam bath, a cold-water pool, a café and an outdoor terrace lounge. As long as you're splurging, pay a bit extra for a fluffy robe. (€16, Mon-Fri 12-15). Open: Mon and Wed-Sat 12-23; Tues 15-23; Sun 13-19. (Map area C4)

nergy Revival Health Company - Nieuwe Nieuwstraat 12, ☎ 625-2985

Led by professor and traditional Chinese doctor Jian Ming Gu, a staff of massage therapists awaits your tired travel muscles – at a very reasonable price. A half-hour foot massage costs €9.50 and a full Chinese body massage is only €14 for a half hour or €28 for an entire hour. An acupuncture session will run you €35. This is a great way to get rid of all your kinks. Open: Daily 11-23. (Map area D4)

swimming pools

uiderbad - Hobbemastraat 26, ☎ 678-1390
0 years old. Beautifully restored. Naked swimming unday afternoon 16:30-17:30. And occasionally, live zz while you do the breast -stroke! (Map area C8)

irandabad - De Mirandalaan 9, ☎ 646-4444
ndoor/outdoor. With whirlpool, wave machine and opical bath. South.

levoparkbad - Zeeburgerdijk 630, ☎ 692-5030
eated outdoor pool. Open mid-May to early Sept. ast.

Bijlmerbad - Bijlmerpark 76, ☎ 697-2501
Disco swimming on Sunday afternoon. South east.

Marnixbad - Marnixplein 9, ☎ 625-4843
Modern. Swimming, fitness, physiotherapy. Centrally located. (Map area B3)

Sloterbad-President Allendelaan 3, ☎ 506-3506
Olympic sized pool, outdoor swimming in summer, indoor kid pool with water slide!

beaches

Zandvoort and the Coast

Trains to Zandvoort (on the coast) leave from Centraal Station approximately every half hour. In summer there are direct trains for the 30-minute trip and on sunny days they're packed. Off-season you have to change trains in Haarlem. Zandvoort can get very crowded, the water makes you shiver and the wind likes to blow. But the beach is big, wide and white, and a day trip there can be a lot of fun. Some Dutch women go topless at any beach, but South of Zandvoort is a section especially for nudists to brown their bodies. If you want to party, Bloemendaal aan Zee is a 45-minute walk north along the beach from Zandvoort. Several pavilions host regular parties, both wild and chilled. Sometimes there's a beach shuttle that'll take you there, but usually you have to hoof it. Remember to check the departure time of the last train back to Amsterdam.

Blijburg - Haveneiland, Ijburg, ☎ 416-0330

www.blijburg.nl

Blijburg is the most beloved Amsterdam beach, a relaxed oasis from the bustling city. They throw parties large and small with eclectic mixes of live music and DJs. The café has a full bar plus fine edibles—their *patatas bravas* with garlic mayo are killer—and the vibe is lively even when the weather's crap. Lots of comfortable nooks and crannies make for great lounging, both inside and on the terraces, or bring your blanket and flake out on the sand. Clean water means you can dip when you desire. It's a bit of a trek by bike, but tram 26 from Centraal Station will take you right there. Open: Daily in summer (not sure about winter).

Het Twiske - North of Amsterdam, near Landsmeer

Het Twiske is a fresh water lake close to Amsterdam with picnic areas, hiking paths and lots of beaches. You can rent canoes, sailboats, kayaks and surfboards. On the east side of the park is a nude beach (Wezenland Strand). By bike it's an easy peddle (bike shops have maps), or take bus 92 from Centraal Station and get off at Kerkbuurt in front of the visitor's center.

street festivals

Queen's Day - April 30, Everywhere in Holland

Amsterdam's craziest street party of the year happens in celebration of Queen Beatrix's birthday – or actually her mother's birthday, because the queen's is in bitter cold January. The city becomes one big orange-colored carnival of music, madness and dancing in the street, plus the world's biggest yard sale is open for business. Streets and canals are packed with people selling clothes, CDs, shoes, bric a brac, microwave ovens, 20-year-old leather jackets… everything imaginable is bought or sold. Despite a ridiculous slew of rules and regulations imposed by the City Council over the last few years, Queen's day is a blast. Type "Queen's Day Amsterdam" into any search engine and you'll find hundreds of photos online.

Bevrijdingsdag - May 5, Museumplein

www.amsterdamsbevrijdingsfestival.nl

Bevrijdingsdag celebrates Holland's liberation from the Nazis at the end of WWII. Festivals happen all around the country and Amsterdam hosts some of Holland's bigger bands, plus a few lesser knowns for free concert on a transformed Museumplein. It's always a fun party. Fuck the Nazis! (Map area B8)

Positive Rave Organization Street Party - Late May-Early June

http://legalize.net

Because the man gets nervous when the streets are liberated, this annual parading street rave protesting the global war on drugs has been forced out of Amsterdam's center and the permit for their famous free after-party cancelled. But the struggle continues – heads and sound-systems still gather every year. Check their website for info about the next event.

Kwakoe Festival - July and August, Bijlmerpark, Amsterdam Zuid-Oost

www.kwakoe.nl

With over half a million visitors, mostly of Surinamese, Antillean and Ghanaian origin, this is Holland's biggest multicultural festival. It takes place over six weekends every summer and admission is free. The soccer games are the biggest draw, but there's also lots of music, food and art. Visit their site or call 416-0893 for details.

Gay Pride Parade - First weekend in August

www.amsterdampride.nl

If you're here at the beginning of August, don't miss this extravagant, risqué boat procession cruising the canals, celebrating gay pride. Amsterdam goes off! Street parties and cultural events, including open-air film screenings, happen over the entire weekend. Call the Gay & Lesbian Switchboard (see Phone Numbers chapter), or stop by Pink Point (see Practical Shit chapter) for route information.

Hartjesdag - Third weekend in August,

Zeedijk and Nieuwmarkt

Hartjesdag dates back to medieval times when citizens would cross dress and party every year at this time. It's a lively weekend culminating with the Zeedijk and the Nieuwmarkt (see Hanging Out chapter) being occupied with partying drag queens and kings.

New Year's Eve - uh...

Coming for New Year's Eve? Want to be at an organized party? Start checking the club and AUB websites at least a month in advance. All the popular venues sell out fast. Thousands of people also celebrate on the streets, especially at Nieuwmarkt (see Public Squares, above). Expect fireworks galore and chaos—madness Amsterdam style!

kids

Traveling with kids is challenging but fun, and like a friend of mine put it: "Not all people with children are squares." Definitely not. Amsterdam, known for its debauchery and mind-twisting tourism, is also a great place for the little ones.

Kids love **pancakes**, and so do the Dutch. You can take a cruise on a pancake boat. De Pannenkoekenboot departs at 16:30 and 18:00, Wed.-Sun. from NDSM werf. Take the ferry behind Centraal Station marked NDSM and 10 minutes later you're there, ready to board a river cruiser for a one-hour pancake-filled munch-out, buffet style. It costs €14.50 for adults and €9.50 for children. They recommend you reserve during the busy summer months at *www.pannenkoekenboot.nl* or call 636-8817.

Another pancake-filled adventure is to visit **Boederij Meerzicht** (*www.boederijmeerzicht.nl*), a waterside farmhouse in a huge park in south Amsterdam called the Amsterdamse Bos where the peacocks and various farm animals will watch you eat. (Buses 170, 172 from Centraal Station.)

hanging out

If you want to eat pancakes or tasty little poffertjes – mini-pancakes with butter and powdered sugar – but remain in the Centrum, check out **De Carousel** (Weteringcircuit 1, tel: 625-8002). It's a big round restaurant with lots of windows and a roomy terrace. Little kids love this place. Big kids too – my editor swears these are the best pancakes in town; he chows down here at least once a week. (Map area C,D8)

Got kids that **ride bikes**? Why not rent a few for the family? Most shops have a variety of sizes and possibilities – like bike seats for toddlers. (See Getting Around.) Bicycle rental shops also have tour maps showing routes to beautiful old villages located just north of Amsterdam.

There's a great **outdoor market** Saturdays at the Noordermarkt (see Shopping, markets) that's got organic munchies, clothing and craft stalls and a playground for kids in the middle.

Museums can be a good rainy-day destination for people with children, and Nemo Science Museum (see Museum chapter) is a perfect example. There are interactive exhibitions especially for children – even a real Tesla ball. If the weather's good, you can eat lunch on the giant rooftop terrace. The Tropenmuseum (see Museum chapter) is fun for children and adults. They have interactive displays of developing countries, including models of villages and fantastic art expositions.

Amsterdam's huge **public library** is another rainy-day possibility with plenty for kids and adults to do and explore (see Hanging Out, Libraries). (Map area F4)

Kid-friendly restaurants can be challenging to find in this city. How about dinner on a boat? At the **Einde van de Wereld**, opposite Javakade 4, on board Quo Vadis, you can eat organic meat or vegetarian meals for a good price. Kids have their own space here to frolic and play (see Restaurants). (Map area I3)

Café Restaurant Amsterdam (Watertorenplein 6, 682-2666) is in the Westerpark neighborhood outside of the Centrum. It's not cheap, but for a special treat this is a fantastic kid-friendly locale. Kids are free to run wild in this huge space, the staff doesn't care at all – even when all 100+ tables are full. The menu is French meets modern and classic Dutch with steaks, fresh seafood and a good selection of vegetarian options. Everything from the bread to the mayonnaise is made in-house. Price-wise, you can go as tame or extravagant here as you desire. Take tram 10 west to the end of the line at Van Hallstraat, walk west two minutes into a square called Watertorenplein (Watertower Plain) surrounded by apartments. The Café is on your left in an old milk factory next to a white water tower. Reservations are recommended on weekends or you'll have to wait a while for a table.

Talia (Prinsenstraat 12, 320-2031) is a fantastic pizza and focaccia shop (see Food, pizza) but they also offer family friendly, authentic Italian three course meals. It's a bit of a splurge and reservations are mandatory, either by phone or at the shop, but they only take up to eight people. So a small family can reserve Talia's beautiful space for a private or small group meal. You can customize the menu and let the chef know exactly what you and your family prefer to eat. Younger kids also get a big discount.

On sunny days **parks** (see this chapter, parks) are always great for kids. Westerpark, located just west of the Centrum, has big open lawns, a kiddy wading pool, plus cafés and restaurants. Woeste Weste, also in Westerpark, is a kids' outdoor paradise with a mini zipline, a creek, shallow ponds and roughly constructed wooden huts. Kids frolic and get dirty while their parents enjoy a drink or two at the café. From Westerpark follow the main bike path past the big lawn then under the railroad tracks…Woeste Veste is immediately on your right. Vondelpark, Amsterdam's busiest, has a huge playground near the Melkhuis café, about a 10-minute walk from the park's main entrance, on the right.

For an old-style **carnival** experience in mid-August go to the *Openhavenpodium* at Java Eiland (see Music Festivals, Music chapter). You'll find plenty of delicious food, funny and entertaining performances, and other attractions for young and old.

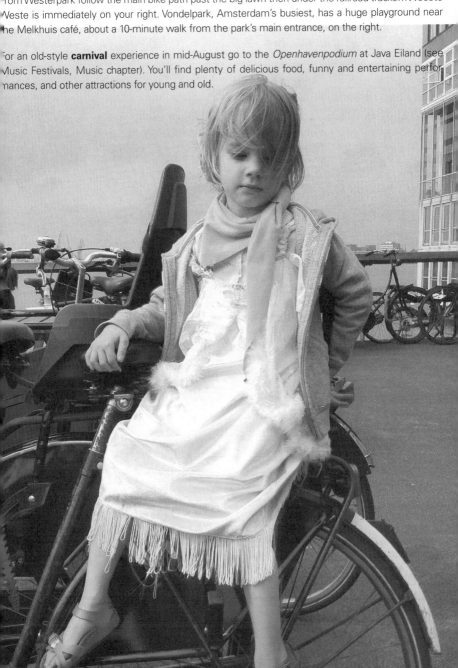

One of Amsterdam's smallest houses

Museums & Galleries

Amsterdam has multitudes of museums and galleries—it's impossible to see even a fraction during an average tourist's stay. *Get Lost!* concentrates on the more unusual or lesser known. Information about the big ones, like the Rijksmuseum and the Van Gogh Museum, is at the end of this chapter. Now for a little strangesness…

the unusual ones

The Sex Museum - Damrak 18, ☎ 622-8376

www.sexmuseumamsterdam.nl

Almost everything displayed here can be seen for free in the Red Light District, but admission is cheap and it's fun to tell friends you checked out the Sex Museum. The exhibits, which were getting pretty run-down, have been restored to their carnal glory. Highlights include pornography from the turn of the century and two 7-foot high penis chairs to can pose on – don't forget your camera! Open: Daily 10-23:30. (Map area E4)

The Erotic Museum - Oudezijds Achterburgwal 54, ☎ 624-7303

The Erotic Museum's collection covers five full floors, but unfortunately much of it is unlabelled. They have drawings by John Lennon, collages from Madonna's Sex, and an ugly, hilarious German porno-toon. Push a button at one display and a dozen vibrators are activated simultaneously. There's a floor with hardcore videos and samples of phone sex, and a rather tame S-M room. Only one reference is made to gay male sex in the entire museum, however – a surprising omission considering Amsterdam's status as Europe's gay capital. Open: Sun-Thurs 11-1; Sat-Sun 11-2. (Map area E4)

The Hash Marihuana Hemp Museum - Oudezijds Achterburgwal 130, ☎ 623-5961

Despite its name, this museum is more than just a required stop on every smoker's list. Their exhibits comprise photos, documents, videos and artifacts dealing with the amazing hemp plant: history, me-dicinal uses, plant-based plastic and cannabis culture. There's even a grow room. They also sell books, magazines and hemp products, including seeds. Visitors who do smoke will be interested in learning about vaporizers: pipes that use a powerful heat source to "vaporize" the THC-bearing resin without ac-tually burning the weed in the bowl. Eagle Bill, who popularized the method and used to vaporize visi-tors here daily, passed away in 2005. Now Joseph, a vaporizer disciple, carries on Bill's tradition. He's sitting at a table by the grow room and will gladly give you a taste for a small donation. The museum is located in the Red Light District. A few doors down is the new Hemp Museum Gallery with great displays, like mid-19th-century medicine bottles with "extract of cannabis Indica: for coughs, colds, bronchitis, asthma, nervous debility etc." The Gallery also sells limited-edition hand-painted posters. One ticket gains you entry to both museum and gallery. Open: Daily 10 -23. (Map area E5)

museums & galleries

Electric Ladyland - The First Museum of Florescent Art - Tweede Leliedwarsstraat 5, ☎ 420-3776
www.electric-lady-land.com

It took seven years to complete this tiny, trippy museum in a Jordaan shop basement. It includes an intricate cave-like environment, a push of a button lights different areas of the space with Jimi Hendri as background music. An international mineral and fluorescent artifact collection is displayed under lights of different wavelengths revealing startling hidden colors. A €5 donation gets you entrance and an informative booklet. Open: Tues-Sat 13-18. (Map area B4)

The Torture Museum - Singel 449, ☎ 320-6642
www.torturemuseum.n

Don't leave Amsterdam without visiting this unique and very educational collection of torture instru ments. You'll learn where expressions like "putting the pressure on" and "going medieval" originated The museum is in an old house and barely illuminated by dingy dungeon lighting. Detailed drawing illustrate each objects purpose, with a small plaque explaining its function and on whom it was used Christianity's bloody history graphically documented. Open: Daily 10-23. (Map area E4)

Tropenmuseum - Linnaeusstraat 2, ☎ 568-8215
www.kit.nl/tropenmuseun

Tropenmuseum (Tropical Museum) is an amazing place—complete with authentic artifacts and de tailed exhibits from the developing world—yet it isn't so popular with tourists. Inside this stunning building, completed in 1920s, are exhibitions with model villages, slide shows, music and lots of push button, hands-on displays to give you a feel for everyday life in these distant lands. At the entrance you'll find info on films and music being presented in the adjoining Souterijn theater (see Film chapter) though they're not included in the admission price. Admission: €9 (Under 18: €5). Open: Daily 10-17 (Map area H7)

De Poezenboot (Cat Boat) - a houseboat on the Singel opposite #20, ☎ 625-8794

Attention cat lovers! This isn't really a museum, but what the fuck. Spend some time on this boat play ing with dozens of love-hungry stray cats that now have a home – thanks to donations from the public and local volunteers. The boat is free to visit, but you're expected to make a contribution on your way out. Grab a postcard for your cat back home. Open: Daily 13-17. (Map area D3)

Woonboot Museum (Houseboat Museum) - Across from Prinsengracht 296, ☎ 427-0750
www.houseboatmuseum.n

The 95-year-old ship housing this museum illustrates what it's like living on one of Amsterdam's ap proximately 2500 houseboats. There are also scale models of other boats, photos, a slide show, and displays to answer questions about life on the canals. If you print the map on their website and bring it along, they'll give you a free poster of Amsterdam. Admission: €3.50, kids €2.75. Open: Mar-Oct Wed-Sun 11-17; Nov-Feb, Fri-Sun 11-17. (Map area C5)

W 139 - Warmoesstraat 139
www.w139.n

This large exhibition space and production facility located on the edge of the Red Light District is oper daily from 11-19:00 and offers free admission as part of its mission "to be as public as the post of fice" – contemporary art for the masses. W 139 exhibits artists from around the world and even hosts fashion shows with singing and guitar-playing models wearing locally-created, one-of-a-kind designs Sometimes there are parties with hip underground bands. It's a cool vibe: You can just walk in and look at unpretentious cutting-edge art or grab some flyers for happening parties in and around the city Check out their website for information on upcoming exhibitions and other activities or even tips or available accommodations for visiting artists. (Map area: D4)

Mediamatic - Vijzelstraat 68-78

www.mediamatic.nl

This massive building once owned by bank behomoth ABN Amro now houses Mediamatic, where new media, art and culture collide. They have exhitbitions like last year's ode to videogames featuring a mass of full size oldies plus first-generation Atari and Nintendo consoles. €5 got you unlimited play! Readings, workshops and various projects are always happening: check their site for specifics or visit their impressive gallery space. (Map area: D7)

Illuseum - Witte de Withstraat 120, ☎ 770-5581

www.illuseum.com

Illuseum is a small freaky gallery, performance space and hangout located in a west-end storefront. Weird, wonderful paintings and sculptures by underground artists are displayed inside dark hallways and rooms. Sometimes they screen movies or have bands jamming in the basement. If the weather's nice, grab a glass of wine or beer and relax in the backyard--it's as uniquely decorated as the rest of the space. And be sure to check out the cool tunnel for resident cats. Open: Wed, Sat, Sun 14-21.

The Chiellerie - Raamgracht 58, ☎ 320-9448

www.chiellerie.nl

Alternative and underground, this little DIY gallery is truly accessible to artists of all stripes. Those so inspired can sign up to be "artist of the week" and have their work featured at a Friday night opening. The shows are fresh and inspiring, drawing a wide range of people who come to mingle and enjoy a drink at the bar. It's a comfortable, shabby, non-commercial space on a gorgeous residential street. Open: Sun, Wed 14-18; Fri 17-22 for the art openings. (Map area E5)

Heineken Brewery - Stadhouderskade 78, ☎ 523-9666

www.heinekenexperience.com

I used to recommend this famous place but the price has gone way up, it's no longer a working brewery, and you don't receive the famous all-you-can drink ending anymore—so it's currently lame to experience the Heineken Experience. Open: Tues-Sun 10-18, with last tickets sold at 17. (Map area D8)

Condom Museum - Warmoesstraat 141, ☎ 627-4174

www.condomerie.com

Housed in a small glass case at the Condomerie (see Sex Chapter) is a colorful assortment of condom packages from around the world. It doesn't take long to view the collection, but checking out the names and slogans on the boxes (like the camouflage condom: "Don't let them see you coming") is good for a few laughs. Open: Mon-Sat 11-17. (Map area D4)

Eddie the Eagle Museum - Tolhuisweg 5

www.eddietheeaglemuseum.com

A creative collective currently housed in the Tolhuistuin (see Music), this museum champions artists of all calibers to dare and fly, like Eddie the Eagle Edwards, Great Britain's famously flawed ski jumper, who came in dead last at the 1988 Calgary Olympics. They exhibit a broad variety of art—genius, compulsive, flawed and fabulous, the impetus to create more important than success. Check their website for upcoming exhibitions and events. (Map area E2)

The Smallest House In Amsterdam - Singel 7

In earlier times, property taxes were based on the width of the house's entrance, so the architects who designed this residence were pretty clever: The front is only 1.01 meters (just over a yard) wide! It's not a museum – people live there – so you can't go inside, but it's still cool to look at while walking by. There are other lilliputian houses in the Centrum, including: Haarlemmerstraat 43 (1.28 meters wide); Oude Hoogstraat 22 (2.02 meters wide); and Singel 166 (1.84 meters wide). (Map area D3)

museums & galleries

Botanical Gardens (Hortus Botanicus) - Plantage Middenlaan 2A, ☎ 625-8411

www.dehortus.nl

Established in 1638, this is one of the world's oldest botanical gardens. Their collection includes thousands of plant species displayed in various greenhouses and landscaped gardens. The largest building has both desert and rain-forest environment–great for warming up on a cold winter day–but my favorite is the stunning palm house. Next to that, in a locked cage, is a Wollemi Pine – a species of tree that dates from the time of the dinosaurs and was thought to be extinct. Peyote grows in the cactus greenhouse, and a visit to the butterfly room should be mandatory. Their café, the Orangerie, is airy, light, and full of plants and little birds hunting for fallen crumbs. Trams: 7, 9, 14. Open: Mon-Fri 9-17; Sat-Sun 10-17 (Dec-Jan 'til 16; Jul-Aug 'til 21). (Map area F6)

De Burcht (National Trade Union Museum) - Henri Polaklaan 9, ☎ 624-1166

www.deburchtvakbondsmuseum.nl

In the late 1800s, the famous architect Hendrik Berlage designed the General Dutch Diamond Cutters Union's head office – the first union in The Netherlands winning its workers the right to a vacation, and the first in the world attaining an eight-hour workday! It's fitting that this monumental building now houses the Dutch trade union movement museum. Most of its exhibits, which include displays about union activities of the past and present, are in Dutch, but a free English guide is available at the front desk. The environment here makes you want to hear some old, scratchy Woody Guthrie albums or sing "Power to the People." Admission is €1.25 for card-carrying union members and €2.50 for the unorganized. Take tram 9 to Plantage Kerklaan. Open: Tues-Fri 11-17; Sun 13-17. (Map area F6)

Museum Het Schip - Spaarndammerplantsoen 140, ☎ 418-2885

www.hetschip.nl

Het Schip (The Ship) is an awesome residential building–curving walls, minaret-like turrets, teardrop and triangular windows–designed in the early 20th century by Michel de Klerk, a member of the famous architectural movement called the Amsterdam School. The museum's collection, located in an ornate corner of the building that used to be a post office, consists of a short film, interactive computer programs and the breathtaking interior itself. You'll learn the Amsterdam School's controversial history and the parallel rise of the social housing movement in Holland. It was radical stuff comrades... and it still is. Take bus 22 from Centraal Station. Admission: €5; students €2. Guided tours cost an extra €2.50 and begin at 13:30. Open: Thurs-Sun 13-17.

FOAM - Keizersgracht 609, ☎ 551-6500

www.foam.nl

Amsterdam's FOAM photography museum is in an old canal house renovated with an open, airy, contemporary style. The exhibitions represent all aspects of the art and change frequently. My museum card and I are regular visitors. Admission is €8, €5 for students. Trams 16, 24, 25. Open: Sat-Wed 10-17; Thurs-Fri 10-21. (Map Area D6)

Huis Marseille Foundation for Photography - Keizersgracht 401, ☎ 539-8989

www.huismarseille.nl

A French merchant built this grand house in the 1600s. It's been restored to its original state and houses a center for photography–the spacious rooms and long hallways perfect for presenting exhibitions. There's also a big library open to the public. Because the building is a monument, it's free to visit on Open Monument Day (see below). Admission: €5 (free for 17 and under). Open: Tues-Sun 11-18. (Map Area C6)

Open Monument Day - Early September, throughout The Netherlands

www.openmonumentendag.nl or www.bmz.amsterdam.nl

On Open Monument Day over 3000 historical monuments in Holland usually not accessible to the public—homes, windmills, courtyards and churches – open their doors. On this day you can pop into any building flying a key-eblazoned flag. For more info call 627-7706 or visit the websites above.

the big ones

Here is some basic information on Amsterdam's biggest and most famous museums. They all have impressive collections and get crowded during peak season. Once a year, in mid-April, there's a Museum Weekend when all the big ones are free. Most of these museums are closed on December 25, January 1, and April 30 (Queen's Day – See Hanging out chapter).

The Museum Nacht (*www.n8.nl*) is a super cool, enormously popular annual happening. For one night in early November over 40 Amsterdam museums are open after hours providing visitors unconventional atmospheres in which to view artwork. Past events included the Stedelijk Museum transformed into a lounge club, line dancing in the Rijksmuseum, and the Botanical Gardens' tour of their hallucinogenic plant collection. More recently, the Nemo had a large Tesla ball sparking synthetic lightning on their famous terrace. The €13.50 Museum Night pass includes entrance to the museums as well as transport on historic trams and buses.

Rijksmuseum - Stadhouderskade 42, ☎ 674-7000

www.rijksmuseum.nl

Still renovating, but one wing is open for viewing their most famous works. Open: Daily 09-18. €10 (18 and under: free). Trams: 2, 5. (Map area C8)

Vincent van Gogh Museum - Paulus Potterstraat 7, ☎ 570-5200

www.vangoghmuseum.nl

Frequently there's free live music or DJ sets in the lobby on Friday nights. Open: Daily 10-18 (Friday 'til 22:00). €12 (ages 13-17, €2.50). Trams: 2, 3, 5, 12. (Map area B8)

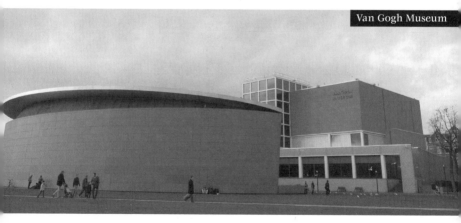

Van Gogh Museum

Anne Frank House - Prinsengracht 263, ☎ 556-7105

www.annefrank.nl

Amsterdam's most visited museum/monument. Book online to avoid long waits in line. Open: Daily 9-19 (Apr-Aug 31 'til 21). €7.50 (ages 10-17: €3.50). Trams: 13, 14, 17. (Map area C4)

museums & galleries

Stedelijk Museum of Modern Art - Oosterdokskade 5, ☎ 573-2911

www.stedelijk.r

You can find this museum's current events online.

Rembrandt House - Jodenbreestraat 4, ☎ 520-0400

www.rembrandthuis.▶

Open: Mon-Sat 10-17; Sun 11-17. Admission: €8; students €5.50; ages 6-15, €1.50. Trams: 9, 1◀ (Map area E6)

Amsterdam Museum - Kalverstraat 92, ☎ 523-1822

www.amsterdammuseum.▶

Formerly the Amsterdam Historical Museum. Open: Mon-Fri 10-17; Sat-Sun 11-17. €10 (ages 6-18, €E Trams: 1, 2, 5. (Map area D5)

Jewish Historical Museum - Nieuwe Amstelstraat 1, ☎ 531-0310

www.jhm.▶

Open: Daily 11-17. €7.50 (ages 13-17: €3). Trams: 9, 14. (Map area E6)

Portuguese Synagogue - Mr. Visserplein 3, ☎ 624-5351

www.esnoga.co▶

Open: Sun-Fri 10-16 (Apr 1-Oct 31); Sun-Thurs 10-16; Fri 10-15 (Nov 1-Mar 31). €6.50 (ages 10-15: €◢ Trams: 9, 14. (Map area E6)

WW2 Resistance Museum (Verzetsmuseum) - Plantage Kerklaan 61, ☎ 620-2535

www.verzetsmuseum.o▶

Open: Tues-Fri 10-17; Sat-Mon 12-17. €6.50 (ages 7-15: €3.50). Tram: 9. (Map area F6)

Willet-Holthuysen Museum - Herengracht 605, ☎ 523-1822

www.willetholthuysen.▶

A 17th-century canal house. Open: Mon-Fri 10-17; Sat-Sun 11-17. Trams: 4, 9, 14. (Map area D6)

Hidden Church (Amstelkring) - Oudezijds Voorburgwal 40, ☎ 624-6604

www.museumamstelkring.▶

Open: Mon-Sat 10-17; Sun 13-17. Admission: €7; students, €5; ages 5-18, €1. (Map area E4)

Maritime Museum (Scheepvaartmuseum) - Kattenburgerplein 1, ☎ 523-2222

www.scheepvaartmuseum.n▶

A museum on an old Dutch ship. €5 for old and young. Docked near NeMo. (Map area G5)

NeMo (Science Center) - Oosterdok 2, ☎ 531-3233

www.e-nemo.▶

Open: Tues-Sun 10-17. €11.50. Bus 22. (Map area F5)

Hermitage Amsterdam - Nieuwe Herengracht 14, ☎ 530-8755

www.hermitage.

Branch of the State Hermitage Museum in St. Petersburg. Open: Daily 10-17. Admission €8 (Under 1 free). (Map area E6)

out of town

Escher In The Palace - Lange Voorhout 74, The Hague, ☎ 070-427-7730

www.escherinhetpaleis.nl

Acid heads tend to have a fondness for M.C. Escher's art and gladly make the 45 minute train ride to this trippy museum, housed in an 18th-century palace. Even non-fryers enjoy Escher's unique vision, from the famous crystal ball self-portrait to repeating pattern drawings like the globe-shaped "Angels and Demons". Paintings, sketches and archive materials are displayed over the museum's four floors. There's also an optical-illusion room that makes you look either like Andre the Giant or about the size of Gary Coleman. And perhaps best of all, a virtual-reality experience where—with the help of a helmet, earphones and a computer—you can go right into one of Escher's paintings! Admission €8. Open: Tues-Sun 11-17.

Kröller Müller Museum - Hoge Veluwe National Park, ☎ 031-859-1041 or ☎ 031-859-1241

www.kmm.nl or www.hogeveluwe.nl

This museum—with a surreal sculpture garden and a fantastic Van Gogh collection—is located in a Dutch national park. Visitors ride complimentary bikes and explore many kilometers of well-maintained paths through orignial forests and sprawling dunes. The park is open during daylight hours; the museum, Tues-Sun 10-17. Admission to the park and the museum is €14; the park alone, €7; parking, €6. There are buses to the museum from the town of Apeldoorn.

Keukenhof - Lisse (southwest of Amsterdam), ☎ 025-246-5555

www.keukenhof.nl

Flower-lovers from around the world converge on this 32-hectare park every spring to see Holland's finest bulbs a-blooming. There are kilometers of grand avenues and winding forest paths, fountains of every size and shape, a Japanese garden, a maze, and many special pavilions for indoor plants – plus over 6 million flowers, most of them tulips. On a sunny day the colors and scents are breathtaking. Don't forget your camera. Getting there involves a train journey to Leiden and then a bus ride through an area filled with commercial bulb fields – also an impressive sight. Admission is €12. Open: Daily 8-19:30 from the end of March 'til mid-May.

Music

Touring bands, both known and obscure, love to play in Amsterdam. Although the number of club and halls isn't numerous, due to bullshit stringent local laws, existing venues—bars, old churches, old dairies, community-run squats, dancehalls—have a fantastic variety of programming. Hip Hop, Punk Rock, Dubstep, Country Rock, Modern Jazz, Reggae—whatever you're into, Amsterdam will satiate your sonic desires.

how to find out who's playing

A.U.B. - Leidseplein 26, ☎ 0900-0191 (40¢ per minute)
www.amsterdamsuitburo.nl

The Amsterdams Uitburo (AUB) is the place to cop tickets for shows at the Paradiso, Melkweg, and other Amsterdam bars and clubs featuring live music (see below). There are also flyer racks and info about theater and film events. It's convenient to buy advance tickets here, in person or by phone, but there's a service charge of about €2 per tic. Buying them directly from venues or record stores (see Shopping chapter) will usually save a little money. Note that you can't buy tickets to concerts at the H******n Music Hall here – you need to go to the post office or the tourist office (see Ticket Service below). Open: Mon-Sat 10-19:30; Sun 12-19:30. (Map area C7)

Last Minute Ticket Shop - Leidseplein 26, ☎ 0900-0191 (40¢ per minute)
www.lastminuteticketshop.nl

Also located in the AUB, the last-minute ticket service offering tickets to concerts, theatre performances, movies and other events at 50% off the regular price. And if you pay cash, there's no service charge. You can see what's available on their site, but you have to buy the tix in person. Open: Daily 12-19:30

Shark
www.underwateramsterdam.com

This popular webzine informs readers what's happening at the best Amsterdam music spots--alternative and mainstream venues. *Daim's Gig Guide* gives you the scoop on who's coming to Amsterdam each month, and the site has a searchable database of current cultural events. They also feature short articles, reviews, horoscopes, and queer info. Check it out.

Irie Reggae Web Site
www.irielion.com/irie

Reggae heads: Check this comprehensive up-to-date listing of reggae bands and sound systems playing around Holland. Forward Jah Jah children!

Ticket Service (sucks) - ☎ 0900-300-1250 (45¢ per minute)
www.ticketmaster.nl

Ticketmaster is a huge international corporate entity using its ticket-service monopoly to rip off live music fans. Sound familiar? These assholes jack up prices in the states as well. But their site will tell you who's playing where and you can order tix for shows that might sell out by the time you arrive. Ticket Crapster also has outlets in the main post offices here and at the Amsterdam Tourist Office at Centraal Station (see Practical Shit chapter).

live music and party venues

Paradiso - Weteringschans 6-8, ☎ 626-4521

www.paradiso.nl

Since hearing Bad Brains *Live at the Paradiso*-- the meanest, leanest live album ever–I always wanted to see this famous venue. So when I first visited Amsterdam I went straight to this legendary spot, a squatted old church transformed into a club. The former pulpit is now the main stage, decorated with original stained glass, and there's a big dance floor surrounded by three balconies. Everyone imaginable – from Willie Nelson to the Roots, Sonic Youth to Parliament/Funkadelic – has played here over the years. Upstairs, a smaller room hosts separate gigs and midnight sets by bands playing directly after the main show. Food is available in the basement, where smaller soirees and DJ sets happen. Crazy parties and performance art are also welcome here: I've seen joint-filled balloons drop from the ceiling and a guy play a slide guitar solo with his dick ensconced in a Jack Daniels bottle while scantily-clad go-go girls held his instrument. Tickets range in price from about €7 for shows in the small hall to €30 for big-name shows on the main stage. There is an additional charge of €2.50 which buys you a membership card that's valid for one month. If you're going to a sold-out concert it's a good idea to purchase your membership card in advance at the AUB to avoid the long line at the door. Both are located a stone's throw from Leidseplein. (Map area C7)

Paradiso

music

Melkweg (Milky Way) - Lijnbaansgracht 234, ☎ 531-8181

www.melkweg.n

The Melkweg – Amsterdam's other classic venue – is housed in a former dairy on a canal near the Leidseplein. Prices, including a membership fee, are about the same as the Paradiso. Bands play in the old hall most nights, or in the bigger, "Max" (shamefully named after its corporate soft-drink sponsor) Melkweg is also famous for surprise or last minute semi-secret shows (Beastie Boys, The Strokes Them Crooked Vultures) where bigger bands grace smaller stages. The café/restaurant Eat at Jo's (see Restaurants, Food chapter) and an adjacent photo gallery are also located on the ground floor; admission to the gallery via the restaurant entrance at Marnixstraat 409 is free from 13 to 20:00 Wednesday thru Sundays. Upstairs there's a video room, a playhouse for live theater (which is often performed in English), and a cinema (see Film chapter). Flyers listing Melkweg events are available by the front door of the club (even when it's closed). The box office is open from 19:30 on every night that there's a show and: Mon-Fri 13-17; Sat-Sun 16-18. (Map area C7)

OCCII (Onafhankelijk Cultureel Centrum In It) - Amstelveenseweg 134, ☎ 671-7778

www.occii.or

This cool squat club has been open for more than 25 years. There's always something going on here live music from thrash to African, queer underground dance nights, cabarets, readings and other happenings. Their small hall has a bar, a nice-sized stage and a dance floor– a comfortable, divey atmosphere. Near the entrance an old stairway leads to the Kasbah café, a more intimate room with smaller events and daytime shows. Look for posters advertising their happenings or wander by. It's part of complex called the Binnenpret (http://binnenpret.org) that also houses a sauna (see Sauna, Hangin Out chapter), a restaurant (see MKZ, Food chapter) and Café de Bollox. It's located at the far side of Vondelpark, across the street and to the left. They usually close for a while in the summer. Tram 2.

OT301 - Overtoom 301, ☎ 779-4913

squat.net/overtoom30

OT301 used to be a film academy and was falling into decay until squatters occupied, remodele and pumped energy into creating a happening space for the masses. Despite pressure from asshol speculators who would rather see this building rot than be used for non-profit purposes, volunteer have managed to create one of Amsterdam's most important counter cultural centers. New project are launched all the time: There's a restaurant/bar (see De Peper, Food chapter), a movie theater (see Film chapter), a darkroom and printing press, and studios used for radio, dance, performances an workshops. There are also some great parties happening in both the restaurant and the big studios DJs play regular gigs plus cool local and international bands (like the Evens) play shows here. OT30 is underground Amsterdam at its accessible best. Look for their schedule online or pick one up at the AUB (see above). Tram 1. (Map area A7)

H******n Music Hall - Arena Boulevard 590, ☎ 409-7900

www.heinekenmusichall.r

Since we have no real say where our tax euros go, funding for this huge music hall was left to a co poration. Enter Heineken. The idea was to bring bands to Amsterdam that draw more people than the city's clubs can handle – and it's doing just that. The problem is that it sucks. It's a big, cold, undeco rated box with absolutely no soul, but having said that, they still book some damn good shows – Pixies Queens of the Stone Age, Nick Cave, Black Keys, Mos Def et al – so it's worth checking out who playing while you're in town. It's located southeast by the Amsterdam Arena stadium: From Centra Station take Metro 54 (direction Gein) to Bijlmer station; from there it's just a two-minute walk.

Maloe Melo - Lijnbaansgracht 163, ☎ 420-4592

www.maloemelo.r

They call this dive the "home of the blues," but you're just as likely to catch bands playing punk, cour try, cajun or rockabilly. It's Amsterdam's most American roadhouse kind of joint. There's live music her every night, often with no cover. When there is, it's usually €5 or less. Walk to the back of the bar and you'll find the entrance to another room where live music happens. This is a good spot to check out local talent, though occasionally they pull in some big names – like the Patti Smith band playing acoustic! If the band is bad, you can always wander next door and see what's happening at the Korsakoff (see Bars chapter). The bar is open from 21:00 (music room from 22:30) until 3 on week nights and 4 on the weekends. Trams: 7, 10, 13, 17. (Map area B5)

Winston International - Warmoesstraat 123-129, ☎ 623-1380

www.winston.nl

All sorts of great stuff happens at this art hotel (see Hotels, Places to Sleep chapter) and nightclub: parties, poetry, art exhibitions and live music seven nights a week. They program everything from lounge nights to hip-hop to punk rock to cabaret. The Winston is also the home of long-running events that have a great reputation and draw loyal regulars, such as the drum'n bass night Cheeky Mondays. The space has been redecorated with a quality sound system, fantastic murals, a wall covered in old speakers, and a multi-functional back-stage room with a remote-controlled sliding wall. It's definitely one of the cooler places in the Red Light District. Cover is usually €5-€7. The entrance is just to the right of the hotel. Open: Sun-Thurs 20-3; Fri-Sat 20-4. (Map area D4)

Bimhuis - Piet Heinkade 3, ☎ 788-2150

www.bimhuis.nl

Amsterdam's most famous jazz club is in the Music Building (Muziekgebouw), about a 20-minute walk east along the water from Centraal Station. Go in the front doors and the Bimhuis is up the stairs to the left. The performance space and café has a sterile feeling though it still retains a little bit of the intimacy of the old location. The sound quality, however, is excellent. Ticket prices average €10 to €20 and some super-hot musicians play here. There are also regular free events like Tuesday night jams, late night dancing to rare grooves, and laptop/turntable sessions. Concerts at the Bimhuis start at 21:00. From Centraal Station take tram 26 to the first stop east. (Map area G3)

music

Pacific Parc - Polonceaukade 23, Cultuurpark Westergasfabriek

www.pacificparc.nl

Pacific Parc is one of Amsterdam's cooler venues. Bands and DJs perform at this club/café Thursday through Sunday weekly. I saw garage-rock one-man-band gurus King Khan and BBQ performing here together for free (that's a nice price). Local DJ Bone and his trail of bands are regulars. He's known to spin a melange of '60s punk and garage, raw rockabilly, old school hip-hop and skuzzy-sounding beat. Located in Westerpark (see Hanging out) at the Westergasfabriek (see this chapter below). (Map area A1)

Sugar Factory - Lijnbaansgracht 358, ☎ 627-0008

www.sugarfactory.nl

The Sugar Factory is a small and nicely laid out space that's hip but unpretentious. They present all kinds of music, theater and film, often in an intriguing mix. This is the home of Wicked Jazz Sounds whose Sunday night parties have become legendary. Right across the alley from the Melkweg (see above). (Map area C7)

Bitterzoet - Spuistraat 2, ☎ 521-3001

www.bitterzoet.com

The crazy antics of the Drugs Peace House squat once housed in this building are long gone, but this intimate club's organizers ensure hip happenings seven nights a week. A great mélange of bands and DJs do their thing here–or check their theater where innovative performances are staged. And you can use the upstairs pool table for free! It's just a few minutes walk from Centraal Station. Open: Sun-Thurs 20-3; Fri-Sat 20-4. (Map area D3)

Pakhuis Wilhelmina - Veemkade 576, ☎ 419-3368

www.cafepakhuiswilhelmina.nl

Bands and DJs play nightly as this eastside, waterfront venue– bluegrass, rock, funk, country, live karaoke…whatever. The small stage contributes to the intimacy and attitude-free atmosphere but the sound system kicks serious ass. It's close to the Music Building (see Bimhuis, above) and De Cantine (see Bars chapter). From Centraal Station take tram 26 to Rietlandpark, then cross the busy street and walk to the water. The entrance is at the top of the small staircase in the middle of the Wilhelmina artist warehouses.

Studio K - Timorplein 62, ☎ 692-0422

www.studio-k.nu

This huge space in Amsterdam's *Indische buurt* in the east is a live-music venue, movie theater, community arts center and café. Currently, Monday night has *Gekkenhuis* (fools house) with DJs spinning "hip-hop, funk, soul etc." – and entrance is free. They also have unknown bands and singer/songwriters who perform here to gain exposure. Check out their site for more info. Located just around the corner from the new Stay Okay hostel (see Places to Sleep). Camping Zeeburg is not far away. (Map area J7)

Tolhuistuin - Tolhuisweg 5

www.tolhuistuin.nl

Formerly a control room for Shell Oil in North Amsterdam, and one of the Netherland's most tightly secured buildings, the art deco style Tolhuistuin (literally, toll house garden) is now an artists' coop that's "..an ode to the unconventional." They have an open bar and café, plus an intimate stage where some of the city's finest under and overground bands perform. Local duo Saelors played a free concert last time I visited, mesmorizing a devoted crowd. Drinks are cheap (red or white homemade sangria €2.50) and their food options change regularly. Artists can rent workspace for €15 a day and they offer exhibition space at their Eddie the Eagle Museum. (See Museum chapter.) Psychedelic folk, African hi-life, raw surf punk multi media and video presentations, a light and sculpture garden…Tolhuistuin's eclectic programming deftly mixes musical and art genres– a true bonus to Amsterdam's famous alternative culture. Take the short three-minute ferry behind Centraal Station to Buiksloterweg. Go straight 200 meters, passing another art deco building (the Tolhuis) and a small parking lot, the entrance is on your left. (Map area E2)

The Waterhole - Korte Leidsedwarsstraat 49, ☎ 620-8904

www.waterhole.nl

Tucked away in a little side street off the Leidseplein, this old-school bar has cheap drinks and live music. Bands play every night starting at about 22:30 and there's never a cover charge. It's a rock-and-blues-covers jam-session kind of place. There are a few pool tables in the back. Happy hour is from 18-21. Open: Sun-Thurs 16-3; Fri-Sat 16-4. (Map area C6)

Goth Stuff - Various Locations

Check the Kagen site (www.kagankalender.com) for listings of goth and goth-related parties and concerts all over Holland and Belgium. It's in Dutch but easy to figure out. Another useful site updated regularly is www.gothicnederland.nl. The infamous Bal du Masque parties are amazing costume affairs with absinthe bars, satanic puppet shows, sexy bands and people dressed in authentic Renaissance garb. These parties always sell out, so check out www.baldumasque.nl for details and advance tickets.

King Shiloh Sound System - Various Locations

www.kingshiloh.com

This international roots-reggae sound system has been around for years, throwing parties and operating a recording studio, a record label and a program on pirate Radio 100 (see Radio, below). They play regular gigs at their home base NDSM, the Paradiso (see above) and after most big reggae shows. Check their website for more info. Stay positive.

Westergasfabriek - Haarlemmerweg 8 10, ☎ 586-0710

www.westergasfabriek.nl

This old factory complex consists of 15 renovated industrial monuments and their surrounding grounds. It's a fantastic site that hosts music and film festivals, parties and performances. There's a music venue (see Pacific Parc above), a movie theatre, a bakery and a couple of restaurants and cafés. There's also lots of expansive parkland popular with picnickers, dog-walkers and stoners tossing frisbees. It's a 30-minute walk from Centraal Station, or take bus 18 or 22. (Map area A1)

Akhnaton - Nieuwezijds Kolk 25, ☎ 624-3396

www.akhnaton.nl

Well-known for its African and Latin American music nights, Akhnaton also features hip-hop techno, dancehall, reggae, and currently, the Kinky Salon fetish parties (see Sex.) Only a five-minute walk from Centraal Station. Open most Friday and Saturday nights. Admission is usually €7 to €10. (Map area D4)

Theater de Cameleon - Derde Kostverlorenkade 35, ☎ 489-4656

www.decameleon.nl

Theater de Cameleon, located in the charming Oude West neighborhood, hosts entertaining non-commercial alternative performances. They present plays, concerts, and improv comedy. Every month there's an open stage with comedy, street theater, performance art—anything is possible. It's an international scene, English is widely spoken, and it's always a laugh. Call ahead if you'd like to perform. Admission ranges from €2.50 on the open-stage night up to €10 for other events. Tram 1. Closed in August.

Ruigoord Festival - June 21 and other dates, Ruigoord

www.ruigoord.nl

For over three decades this squatted village west of Amsterdam has been a cool community of artists and free thinkers. A sleazy harbor development project –an excuse to bury toxic waste! – bulldozed most of the trees and ripped up the land then evicted families living there. There's still a small community of artists occupying, and they host frequent parties – especially on full-moon nights. Their psychedelic outdoor Summer Solstice bash is legendary as are their Landjuweel and Virige Tungen festivals. There is also a café and regular happenings – including drum sessions, poetry readings, Sunday afternoon singer/songwriter and Americana shows – at the old community church, which managed to escape the wrecking ball. For news and directions check their website.

music

ADM - Hornweg 6, ☎ 411-0081

www.admleeft.nl

This huge West-Amsterdam harbor-side building was squatted in 1997 after sitting empty for years. Their opening party featured performances by Bettie Serveert (who played a fantastic set of Velvet Underground covers) and underground legends The Ex. ADM is still here, and they throw fantastic parties and festivals. Sleaze rock, techno, experimental, kletzmer, hardcore…whatever—you can hear it here. In addition to their special events, they also serve a three-course vegetarian meal in their café every Wednesday, Friday and Sunday from 18:00. Because the building's owner is an evil little fucker, the effort to get out here and support the residents will be especially appreciated. If you're not up to the long bike ride, there's usually a shuttle bus that leaves from behind Centraal Station when they have parties. Call in the afternoon to reserve and for directions.

NDSM Werf - T.T. Neveritaweg 15, Amsterdam North, ☎ 330-5480

www.ndsm.nl

After forcibly closing most of the affordable spaces for artists and their audiences in the Centrum, the City Council is now helping to fund this complex on the site of a squatted wharf in North Amsterdam, and it's turned into a happening place. The area is still being developed, but there are already big art and theater festivals here, a fantastic skate-park (see Hanging Out chapter), cafés, galleries, and a big month-ly flea market (see Shopping chapter). There are also plans for more performance spaces, cheap studios and a cinema. A direct ferry leaves regularly from behind Centraal Station and takes about 10 minutes.

Trouw Amsterdam – Wibautstraat 127, ☎ 463-7788

www.trouwamsterdam.nl

Trouw, a former Dutch newspaper office and printing press, has been transformed in one of Amster-dam's coolest venues "…a city within a city." Besides throwing concerts and mega-hip techno parties they have expansive exhibition space, a mediterranean inspired restaurant with decently priced gourmet fare, an independent record label, plus various cosmopolitan art happenings. Visit Trouw to plug into Am-sterdam's buzzing cultural current. Check their site for upcoming events. Located near Amstel Station.

Club 8 - Admiraal de Ruyterweg 56B, ☎ 685-1703

www.club-8.nl

I got schooled the last time I played snooker at this laid-back west-end club, but at least some killer funk kept my ears happy. But whatever the music, it's a cool place to shoot snooker (€9.50/hour) or pool (€8.50/hour), especially for students: for each student who plays a table before 19:30 there's a 25% dis-count, so if four play, it's free! There's also a full bar and a restaurant that serves cheap snacks as well as meals. Up one floor via the completely graffiti-laden stairwell is the rest of the club where they present theater, indie dance nights (Club Rascal), queer parties, and a monthly roller disco (www.krupoek.com) where DJ's spin Nu-Soul, Hip-Hop and R&B. Bring some ID for the skate rental. On Friday nights new-agers gather here for barefoot dance meditation. Tram 13. Open Sun-Thurs 12-1; Fri-Sat 12-3.

Plantage Doklaan - Plantage Doklaan 8

www.plantagedok.nl

There hasn't been too much happening lately at this legalized squat, but the space – especially the big hall – is amazing. Past events here include alternative book fairs, student fashion shows, underground restaurants and some great parties. It's not the kind of place you just drop into, but if you see flyers around town for an event, check it out.

Rijkshemelvaartdienst - Oudehaagseweg 58

www.rijkshemelvaart.com

This space was an old military compound squatted in 1989 now housing studios and living spaces. Occasionally they present art exhibitions and have been known to throw sensational parties—with soundsystems, bonfires, mobile bars and zaniness. They also have a cheap vegetarian restaurant that's open from time to time. In the past they've combined meals with DJs, films and video reruns of The Love Boat. Another squatted terrain in the neighborhood is the Nieuw en Meer (*www.nieuwenmeer.nl*) also an artists' community that sometimes opens its doors to show the residents' work. If you're going to visit out here, make a day of it and explore the Bos. It's tricky to navigate this area, so get directions from one of the websites first.

dance clubs

Clubs usually open at about 23:00 and close around 4 or 5:00. Most have a dress code. A group called Unitelife (*www.unitelife.nl*) sometimes organizes open-house weekends where for a set price (about €20) you can party at over 20 clubs. For underground parties or events at other locations, you can pick up flyers at bars, coffeeshops and record stores around town. Techno, dub step, drum'n'bass, house, electro, trance, hardcore and multi-genre parties are happening frequently, especially in Summer. The Amsterdam Dance Event (*www.amsterdam-dance-event.nl*), one of Europe's biggest dance and electronic conferences, happens in late October. 5 Days off (*www.5daysoff. nl*) is an amazing and diverse dance festival happening in mid July at various local venues.

Air - Amstelstraat 24, ☎ 820-0670 **www.air.nl**

Inclusive. Formerly the legendary IT, now a Club for everyone—underground to chic. Hip hop, disco, techno, house, cutting edge…Some nights, like Cookie Club, admission is free before midnight.

Panama - Oostelijke Handelskade 4, ☎ 311-8686 **www.panama.nl**

Trendy. Also a theater. Good PA here…now they're also booking more bands. Open: Thurs-Sun. (Map area I4)

De Trut - Bilderdijkstraat 156 **www.trutfonds.nl**

Gay (mixed). In a legalized squat. Admission is only €1.50. Sunday nights only. Doors open at 23:00 and close at 23:30. (Map area A6)

Jimmy Woo - Korte Leidsedwarsstraat 18, ☎ 626-3150 **www.jimmywoo.com**

Trendy. Tight door. Open: Wed-Mon. (Map area 7B)

Escape - Rembrandtplein 11, ☎ 622-1111 **www.escape.nl**

Popular, especially on Saturday. Open: Tues-Sun. (Map area E6)

Club Home - Wagenstraat 3, ☎ 620-1375 **www.clubhome.nl**

Trendy. Open: Thurs-Sat. (Map area E6)

Odeon - Singel 460, ☎ 521-8555 **www.odeontheater.nl**

Three floors. Also a concert hall. Open: Thurs-Sun. (Map area C6)

Tonight's - Gravesandestraat 51, ☎ 820-2451 **www.hotelarena.nl**

In the Hotel Arena (see Places to Sleep chapter). (Map area G8)

C.O.C. - Rozenstraat 14, ☎ 623-4079 **www.cocamsterdam.nl**

Gay. Mixed dance on Friday nights. Saturday nights are women only. (Map area C4)

music festivals

Amsterdam and the surrounding area have festivals year round, both indoor and outdoor. Most listed here are free.

Amsterdam Roots Festival - Mid-June, Oosterpark

www.amsterdamroots.nl

Music from every corner of the world has been showcased over the years at this amazing festival. Concerts are staged in several venues around town for which you need tickets—most notably the Melkweg (see above)—but there's always a day of free performances on seven stages in the Oosterpark (see Hanging Out chapter). It's fantastic: there's music, films, Moroccan tea tents, food, and more music. You may see West African funk bands, psychedelic Mali desert groups or Morrocan trance folk music. Definitely try to catch this one. Note: The incompetent Amsterdam City Council that pumps money into ridiculous building schemes has cut funds for the arts. The Roots festival is in jeopardy. Check out their website to give some support or receive updated information.

Park Pop - Late June, Zuiderpark, Den Haag

www.parkpop.nl

Europe's biggest free pop festival happens annually at this park—with over 300,000 music fans in attendance. Every year sees an interesting line-up of diverse performers but you'll have to truck out to The Hague for this one.

African Music Festival - First weekend in August, Delft

www.africanfestivaldelft.nl

Here's another festival outside Amsterdam. It's an incredible feast of African music—some of the continent's best and most famous stars play here. Tickets are about €15 if you buy them in advance. There's camping nearby or you can hop a train back to Amsterdam (they run all night).

Amsterdam Roots Festival

Parade - Mid-August, Martin Luther King Park

www.deparade.nl

As the sun sets at this old-style European carnival, barkers and performers compete to draw you inside circus tents to witness strange, otherworldly spectacles, live slapstick physical theater and all kinds of weird shit. Admission is free until around 17:00 and then it's about €5. Most of the attractions also charge an admission fee, but it's fun just to hang out, drink some wine and people-watch. The park is in south Amsterdam, along the west side of the Amstel River.

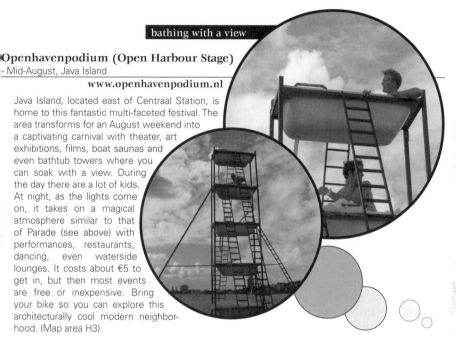

bathing with a view

Openhavenpodium (Open Harbour Stage)
- Mid-August, Java Island

www.openhavenpodium.nl

Java Island, located east of Centraal Station, is home to this fantastic multi-faceted festival. The area transforms for an August weekend into a captivating carnival with theater, art exhibitions, films, boat saunas and even bathtub towers where you can soak with a view. During the day there are a lot of kids. At night, as the lights come on, it takes on a magical atmosphere similar to that of Parade (see above) with performances, restaurants, dancing, even waterside lounges. It costs about €5 to get in, but then most events are free or inexpensive. Bring your bike so you can explore this architecturally cool modern neighborhood. (Map area H3)

Uitmarkt - End of August, in the City Centrum

www.uitmarkt.nl

To celebrate the beginning of the new cultural season, Amsterdam's streets overflow with theater, dance, film and live music. King Sunny Adé, Redman, and Dick Dale have all played big outdoor shows in past years. Almost all the events are free.

Seven Bridges Jazz Festival - Early September, Reguliersgracht

www.sevenbridges.nl

Amsterdam's youngest jazz fest is a one-day affair bringing together Dutch and international groups—and it's free. The stage floats on a canal famous for its picturesque seven-bridges view. (Map area D7)

Gospel Festival - Early September, CEC ebouw, Bijlmerdreef 1289 (Amsterdam Zuid-oost)

www.gospelfestival.nl

This annual event features a wide range of local and international musicians bringing diverse styles to a weekend of musical praise. Past headliners include the mighty Solomon Burke.

musicians

Travelling musicians can rent rooms, for instance with a drum kit, for discount prices. The Jam (Haarlemerweg 315, 682-2877) has several fully equipped rooms available for individual rehearsal or with a band. They cost €10 an hour for a full band and €3-€4 an hour for solo sessions. A drum kit, PA and amps are included. MuzyQ (Atlantisplein 1, 462-5950) is Europe's largest rehearsal studios. They have great gear (including Yamaha drum kits, plus Marshal and Ampeg amps) and the rooms are similarly priced to other rehearsal rooms. Located near Oosterpark (East Park).

Need a van? Bands touring Holland, or anywhere in Europe, can catch a sweet deal on a fully equipped, 6 person Mercedes Maxi van with: 5.1 surround sound, flat screen tv, a refrigerator, a 220v power outlet, DVD, GPS and a queen-size bed. Check out *www.maxisound.nl* .

If you're an Amsterdam transplant in need of some gear check out *www.markplaats.nl*–the dutch version of ebay. You can score some great deals on instruments here.

street performance

Leidseplein and Dam Square are the two main spots for catching break-dancing, juggling acts, living statues and other street shows. If you're a street artist, these two squares are the places to perform during the summer. Leidseplein can get crowded with groups waiting to do their acts, and sometimes a mafia mentality takes hold--it can be difficult to get a slot from the regulars. Street music is basically acoustic instruments only and no drums of any kind. The cops can be real uptight about these rules and sometimes ask for a permit. Noordermarkt on Saturdays and Mondays is a great place to busk if you have a small acoustic act.

underground radio

Radio Patapoe - 88.3 FM

http://freeteam.nl/patapoe

Power to the pirates! Patapoe has been broadcasting diverse programming over Amsterdam airwaves since 1989. Most afternoons and evenings (and 24/7 online) they play all kinds of cool music, from psychedelic underground to industrial lounge to the excellent "Punk as Fuck" hardcore show on Friday afternoons. All with no commercials. Yes!

Radio de Vrije Keyser - 96.3 FM

www.vrijekeyser.nl

Born out of the late-1970s' radical squat movement, these old-time ether pirates became famous for their diverse, sometimes crazy programming. They send a mix of politics, squat news and punk music every Tuesday from 12 to 20:00, and they're often on the scene, broadcasting live from demonstrations and squat evictions around Amsterdam.

Radio 100

www.desk.nl/~radio100

Long live Radio 100: Free the airwaves! Until they were forced off the air by greedy dumbfucks who believe Amsterdam needs only shitty commercial stations, this pirate broadcaster was the city's biggest independent radio station. They've now merged with on-line partner DFM and continue to stream a wide range of shows via internet-- covering diverse subjects and sounds.

Radio Free Amsterdam

www.radiofreeamsterdam.com

This on-line radio station broadcasts a growing number of shows produced in Amsterdam. They include the *John Sinclair Radio Show*, for which the famous activist, former manager of the MC5, musician, blues scholar and "Hardest Working Poet in Show Business" (and our editor) travels the world recording shows with killer tunes and an eclectic variety of interviews.

BBC World Service - 648AM

www.BBC.co.uk/worldservice

It's not exactly alternative, but they do have news in English every hour on the hour.

Bars

Iet Blauwe Theehuis (The Blue Teahouse) - Vondelpark, ☎ 662-0254

www.blauwetheehuis.nl

This circular spaceship of a building is docked in the Vondelpark (see Hanging Out chapter). If it's sunny, the outdoor terrace is packed all day with people sipping drinks and soaking up rays. There's a full bar, they serve snacks from 9 to 16:00, and there are complete meals after that. The bar upstairs opens in the late afternoon—a great treetop perch to watch the sun slowly set. Occasionally there's live jazz upstairs, and on the weekends DJs play anything from rare grooves to soul to Afrobeat. Note that if you stay 'til closing and the park is deserted it's best not to wander about on your own, however tempting a moonlit stroll might be. Open: daily 9-24, though if it's busy on the weekends they sometimes stay open until 3. (Map area A8)

Café the Minds - Spuistraat 245, ☎ 623-6784

www.theminds.nl

This is a legendary bar with a lot of character – like the collection of combat boots hanging from the ceiling – that's located not far from Dam Square. They have a pool table (only 50 cents!), a good pinball machine (5 balls), and punk rock rules the stereo. It's a fun place to hang out and have a drink (beer is €1.25) but weekends get jammed packed with shadowy clad suburban kids. The Minds is also known amongst an (in)famous array of touring punk and rock musicians. Open: Daily 21-3 (or until the owner decides to close.) (Map area D5)

Nieuwe Anita - Frederik Hendrikstraat 111

www.denieuweanita.nl

You have to ring a doorbell to enter this squatted hot spot, but once inside it's like drinking in someone's cozy living room. There's a semi-circular bar featuring cheap drinks and plenty of comfy couches. They have a larger back room for bands and parties. The Big Lebowski Night – complete with a movie screening, White Russians and even virtual bowling – and other Theme Parties happen here. You can also catch some of the city's finest established and new underground bands. The Nieuwe Anita is located west, just outside the city center. (Map area A4)

bars

Jet Lounge - Groen van Prinstererstraat 41, ☎ 684-9888

www.jetlounge.r

Jet Lounge is Amsterdam's finest cocktail bar—a comfortable café with no pretentions. Thank Buddh
that they've found a new west-side location after having to shut their doors for a while, because the
margaritas, shaken on the rocks, are unbeatable! A friend of mine swears by another potion, the Ra
ing Alcoholic, made with various sorts of rum, orange and pineapple juice and served in a paper ba
wrapped bottle. This is a friendly joint, where the American owner is always willing to demonstrate h
customized California-style cocktail-mixing skills. Music ranges from '80s indie/punk to whatever fi
the mood. Jet Lounge showcases local and international singer-songwriters and acoustic bands fiv
nights a week. DJs spin various styles 'til late , but no euro-trash-house allowed! Open Tues-Thur
18-1 Fri.-Sat. 18-3 (Map Area C4)

De Zotte - Raamstraat 29, ☎ 626-8694
www.dezotte.nl

This Belgian bar has 130 Belgian beers and on
its menu, including Trappist monk brewed ales.
The staff is cool and the music last time I was
here ranged from Blondie to the Strokes. It's a
loud and fun place that also serves food – veggie
meals, steaks, homemade Belgian fries, Trappist
cheese plates – nightly from 18-21:30. Food prices
are pretty reasonable, starting at around €8,50. De
Zotte is conveniently located just around the corner
from the Melkweg (see Music) and is a great place
to enjoy a nice strong brew before heading to a gig.
Open: Daily 16-1; Weekends 16-3 (Map area B6)

Batavia - Prins Hendrikade 85

This roomy Dutch bar/café can be found next to the Gothic-style church just across from Centraal Station. The place has two levels complete with a smoking lounge where you can kick back, puff a spliff or a smoke and look out of the big windows over one of Amsterdam's oldest canals. The massive wooden bar was actually delivered in pieces from another Dutch city, reassembled and made into a beautiful piece of work. Batavia has a good selection of bottled beers and sub-zero Jaegermeister on tap. They also offer a full breakfast, lunch and dinner menu plus homemade soups and pies. Sometimes they throw big parties with bands and DJs, like their infamous Halloween bash. (Map area E4)

Beer Temple - Nieuwezijds Voorburgwal 250, ☎ 627-1427

Feel like drinking a Pumpernickel Porter? How about a Punk IPA? These and (give or take) 128 other American microbrews are available at the unique Beer Temple, Europe's first Yankee beer bar. They sell bottles, pints, half pints and even shots of beer ranging in strength from 4.8% to a whopping 50%. Some of the specialty boutique beers sell for up to €20 per bottle, but 30 beers on tap and some fine west coast bottled ales aren't so harsh on the wallet. The interior is comfortable Americana—diner booths and well- stuffed lounge chairs—meets modern bar design. Chalkboards advertise two walls worth of choices so feel free to take your time. And make sure you have a couple of samples before committing! De Arend's Nest (Herengracht 90, map area C4) is another beer bar owned by the same hop-soda obsessives as the Beer Temple-- only all the handcrafted 100+ brews are Dutch. Open: Mon-Thurs 16-1; Fri-Sat 16-2; Sun 14-22. (Map Area C5)

Weber - Marnixstraat 397, ☎ 622-9910

This sometimes overly crowded bar can seem claustrophobic, but take a peek downstairs and you'll find a basement room decked out with old couches, big armchairs, candles and a little greenhouse. You'll find room here to drink a few and shoot the shit with some friends. Open: Sun-Thurs 20-3; Fri-Sat 'til 4. (Map area B7)

Lux - Marnixstraat 403, ☎ 422-1412

This funky place is just a few doors down from Weber and similar in style. DJs play here several nights a week, spinning eclectic digital styles. Open: Sun-Thurs 20-3;Fri-Sat 'til 4. (Map area B7)

Hunter's Bar - Warmoesstraat 35, ☎ 627-9732

www.hunters-coffeeshop.com

A weed smoking friendly pub, Hunter's allow you to enjoy a pint and a spliff, something most bars strenuously dicourage. This policy can be dangerous if you're a rookie–alcohol and cannabis don't always mix—but experienced partiers love the freedom to partake of both. Hunter's also has two coffeeshops on this same stretch with huge hash and weed menus.
(Map area D4)

Belgique - Gravenstraat 2, ☎ 625-1974

www.cafe-belgique.nl

This tiny popular bar has eight beers on tap and more than 30 bottled – specializing in Belgian brews. A local and expat crowd regularly spills out on the tiny old alley where Belgique is located. It gets packed! Street artists, such as the London Police, paint the outside walls with some incredible pieces. Located off the Nieuwendijk, a five-minute walk from Centraal Station or the Dam. Open: daily 15-1 (Map area: D4)

bars

De Koe (The Cow) - Marnixstraat 381, ☎ 625-4482

www.cafedekoe.n

De Koe (The Cow) is an unpretentious joint – a warm, pleasant place to escape the crowds of nearby Leidseplein and hear some blues or rock. On Sunday afternoons they have live music from 16 to 18:00. There are backgammon sets and other games in the front and they serve inexpensive meals down stairs after 18:00. Open:Sun 15-3; Mon-Thurs 16-1; Fri-Sat 16-3. (Map area B7)

Soundgarden - Marnixstraat 164, ☎ 620-2853

An old school Amsterdam punk rock bar, filled with an array of scuz-lovin' dudes and chicks, students expats, German beer lovers--all kinds of people drop in for a night of drinking, table football, pool, dart and pinball. Comfy chairs are scattered about, and the canal side terrace out back is a great spot t smoke a joint and have a real Bavarian wheat beer in the summertime. DJs regularly play surf, ska punk, garage rock, etc. and Soundgarden occasionally has live bands. Open: Sun 15-1; Mon-Fri 13-1 Sat 15-3. (Map area B5)

Brouwerij 't IJ - Funenkade 7, ☎ 622-8325

www.brouwerijhetij.nl

Those of you visiting Amsterdam for a brief stay can fulfill two tourist essentials at once: drink a Dutch beer other than Heineken and see a windmill. The Brouwerij (brewery), built into an ancient bath-house next to the old mill, sells its delicious draft (with alcohol content up to 9 percent!) to a grate-ful crowd of regulars. They also brew a 100% or-ganic white beer and several seasonal beers. On sunny days when the terrace is packed, take your glass across the street, grab a spot at the edge of the canal, and dangle your feet. It's a bit out of the center, not far from the Dappermarkt (see Markets, Shopping chapter) and the Tropenmuseum (see Muse-ums chapter). Open: Wed-Sun 15-20. (Map area H6)

Festina Lente - Looiersgracht 40, ☎ 638-1412

www.cafefestinalente.n

Festina Lente is a popular local bar/café with a full kitchen, a cozy wooden interior and a mellow cana side terrace. There has been a café here for more than 100 years—once called the Bohemia, this wa a wicked jazz bar where Chet Baker and other heavyweights jammed on a miniscule stage. Weekend get jam packed here—mainly Amsterdammers but also a few cooler, more adventurous tourists...lik *Get Lost* readers. Open: Mon 12-1; Tues-Thurs 10:30-1; Fri-Sat 10:30-3; Sun 12-1. (Map area B6)

Korsakoff - Lijnbaansgracht 161, ☎ 625-7854

www.korsakoffamsterdam.n

The Korsakoff is always fun if you're looking to dance to pop-punk, raucous rock, industrial, metal an the odd tune by Prince. Traditionally, a fairly young crowd comes here and weekends get packed. Bu there's music every night (Tuesday nights currently feature techno parties run by the InDeep 'n' Danc crew), drinks are cheap, and upstairs is another cool bar for hanging out and listening to some tunes Buzz to get in. Open: Sun-Tues 23-3; Wed-Thurs 10-3; Fri-Sat 10-4. (Map area B4)

Kashmir Lounge - Jan Pieter Heijestraat 85-87, ☎ 683-2268

The Kashmir Lounge's interior is adorned with Indian metal-work lampshades, embroidered fabrics and colored-glass candle holders--one incense-drenched room is has patterned carpets, pillows deco rated with mirrors, and low wooden tables. This place was a bar/coffeeshop until the city banned the sale of weed and alcohol in the same establishment. It's still smoker-friendly – you can bring your own or grab a bag across the street at one of the tiny neighborhood coffeeshops. DJs play from time to time and then the place gets pretty packed. There's a little terrace out front that opens in the summer. Kashmir Lounge is located not too far from the Ten Kate Market (see Shopping chapter). Open: Mon-Thurs 10-1; Fri-Sat 10-3; Sun 11-1. (Map area C6)

Kingfisher - Ferdinand Bolstraat 24, ☎ 671-2395

Located in a happening district called *De Pijp* (pronounced Pipe), the Kingfisher is an ideal place to plop your ass down and rest after exploring the neighborhood. It's a casual, comfortable place to linger over a light meal and a drink. And at night, when the alcohol starts flowing, it becomes a lively local bar. Open: Sun 12-1; Mon-Thurs 11-1; Fri-Sat 11-3. (Map area C8)

Getto - Warmoesstraat 51, ☎ 421-5151

www.getto.nl

This queer hangout is very different from the famous leather bars that share this strip of the Red Light District. It's a restaurant/bar that's decked out in an arty, comfortable style and it draws a fashionable mixed crowd. In fact, in stark contrast with other bars in the area, there are probably more women here than men. Occasionally Getto has special theme nights, and anytime there's bingo expect a full house. Getto is open: Tues-Thurs 16-1; Fri-Sat 16-2; Sun 16-24. (Map area E4)

Café The Zen - Mollukenstraat 2

You'll find this splendid bar/café located east in the Indische neighborhood. Reggae is the music of choice here as well as jazz and soul; Friday nights DJs spin and it can get packed with locals. The back room, called the Zenergy Lounge, is extremely smoker friendly, joints and cigarettes can be leisurely puffed. They have authentic homemade Surinamese food (dish of the day for €7.50) as well as delicious sandwiches starting at €2.50. Café Padre is located around the corner from Stay Okay (see Hostels) and Studio K (see Film, Live Music). This spot is a great stop if you're heading from Camping Zeeburg to the Center, as it's located en route. Drop by and say hello to Maurits, the super cool owner, settle in and experience some real Amsterdam vibes. Be assured you will be the only tourist, except perhaps another Get Loster. (Map area J6)

Lime - Zeedijk 104, ☎ 639-3020

Lime is a nice bar to lounge with a few friends or have an intimate tet a tet conversation and a drink or two – especially earlier in the evening before it gets crowded. The well-designed interior and arty decor make the space feel bigger than it is, and fresh, like the name. Open: Sun-Thurs 17-1; Fri-Sat 17-3. (Map area E4)

De Buurvrouw - St Pieterspoortsteeg 29, ☎ 625-9654

www.debuurvrouw.nl

As well as booking local bands (usually acoustic so the neighbors don't complain), this bar also features DJs, organizes pool tournaments and hosts open stage nights for stand-up comedy, music and poetry. De Buurvrouw is decorated in an arty mish-mash of styles and one wall is regularly used to display new works. It's a hopping late-night spot that overflows with student types on the weekends. Open: Mon-Thurs 21-3;Fri-Sun 21-4. (Map area D5)

De Duivel (The Devil) - Reguliersdwarsstraat 87

The Duivel was Amsterdam's first hip-hop bar. Over the years they've kept to their roots, though don't be surprised if their DJs throw in a little funk here or some dub there. The space is small and dark and on the weekends it can get uncomfortably crowded, but the vibe is always cool. Yes, yes y'all. Open:Sun-Thurs 20-3;Fri-Sat 'til 4. (Map area D6)

bars

Diep - Nieuwezijds Voorburgwal 256, ☎ 420-2020

Diep, just around the corner from Dam Square, is a cool little bar where anything can happen: crazy nights or lazy nights, jam sessions, barbeques, DJs of every level and style and local hipster spotting. Out front, weather permitting, there's a bustling terrace. It's popular with Amsterdammers, thus a good place to observe or mingle with the native wildlife. (Map area C5)

Barney's Uptown - Haarlemmerstraat 105, ☎ 427-9469

www.barneys.biz

This joint friendly bar/restaurant has taken the breakfast from the famous Barney's Breakfast Bar, the latter still a popular coffeeshop across the street. They serve pancakes and full breakfasts well into the afternoon. At night the fully stocked bar is a relaxing place to have a drink and a spliff. 90s New school hip-hop was the music *du jour* last time I visited, but everything from reggae to Hendrix is possible. DJs regularly spin here and they have various parties and nights happening (check their website). (Map area D2,3)

Vakzuid - Olympisch Stadion 35, ☎ 570-8400

www.vakzuid.nl

The 1928 Olympics were held in Amsterdam and the stadium built for the occasion now houses a restaurant/bar instead of a javelin throwers lounge, or whatever used to occupy this red brick monument's south side. The food's too expensive for me – actually, so are the drinks – but I love the lounge downstairs. With its low, comfortable couches and fake fireplaces, it looks like a 1970s suburban den, and the view of the track and field is awesome. There are DJs a few nights a week, but for truly relaxed lounging I recommend weekday afternoons when the place is almost empty. In the summer there's a cushy terrace out front – ideal for recovering from the long bike ride out here. Open: Mon-Thurs 10-1; Fri 10-3;Sat 12-3; Sun 12-1.

Sappho - vijzelstraat 103, ☎ 423-1509

www.sappho.nl

Sappho, a lively women's bar located in a little storefront, is on a rather desolate stretch of Vijzelstraat. Early in the evenings it can be a bit desolate inside as well, but usually the DJs have the joint jumping by 11 o'clock – especially at their popular Friday night events. Open: Sun, Tues-Thurs 18-1; Fri-Sat 18-3. (Map Area D7)

Café Saarein 2 - Elandsstraat 119, ☎ 623-4901

www.saarein.nl

This famous old-school dyke bar was one of the first women-only spaces in town. It's still a gay café but also caters to a mixed clientele. The neighborhood and the building are both beautiful—Sarein is a pleasant stop for a meal, a beer or a game of pool. Open: Sun-Thurs 17-1;Fri-Sat 17-2. (Map area B5)

Gollem - Raamsteeg 4, ☎ 330-2890

www.cafegollem.nl

With over 200 mostly Belgian beers in stock, even the most serious beer lovers will be able to find one they've never tasted. Lists of what's available, including some beers that are exclusive to Gollem, are posted on blackboards around the pub. There are 10 beers on tap, and each brand of beer is served in a special glass. The bar itself is comfortable but a bit ramshackle and also quite small; visit early if you want to avoid crowds. Or you can check out their other bar in De Pijp neighborhood (Daniel Stalpertstraat 74). Gollem is very popular with locals and tourists alike, and you might spot the odd beer-brewing Trappist monk in the house, silently checking out the competition. Open: Sun 14-1; Mon-Thurs 16-1; Fri-Sat 14-3. (Map area C5)

De Cantine - Rietlandpark 373, ☎ 419-4433

www.decantine.nl

The Canteen was once a squat, one of many in this neighborhood. Now it's a stylish café that serves snacks and full meals, though I like stopping in for beer and whiskey on Sunday afternoons when there's live music. Bands start at 16:00 and play anything from jazz to Americana to rock. On Friday nights DJs spin cool and funky tunes until the wee hours. The decor here is clean and simple – the space is also used for art exhibitions – but not cold. They have free wireless internet and, in warm weather, a pleasant terrace out front. It's right across the street from the Lloyd Hotel (see Places to Sleep chapter). Open: Sun-Thurs 11-1;Fri-Sat 11-3. (Map Area I4)

Azart (Ship of Fools) - KNSM Eiland

www.azart.org

This old ship and its performing crew have been in *Get Lost!* since the very first edition. Since then the artists on board have spent years sailing the world, but they always come back to Amsterdam and dock on KNSM Eiland. When they're here, the bar opens once or twice a week around 22:00 and the fun begins. There's usually live music, plays, poetry, dancing and anything else the residents dream up during the week. It's a little grungy – the toilet's only for women and guys are expected to pee off the edge of a plank into the water (it feels great!) – but the atmosphere is fun and welcoming. It's a bit of a trek out here, so you might want to combine it with dinner at End of the World (see Restaurants, Food chapter). Ride your bike or take bus 42 from Centraal Station (direction KNSM Eiland) or night bus 359 (ask the driver to let you off at Azartplein). (Map area J3)

PINT Bock Beer Festival - Late October, Beurs van Berlage, Damrak 277

www.pint.nl/pint/bbf.htm

Beer lovers gather every October for this three-day beer celebration of bock beer, a traditional lager brewed at the end of harvest season. PINT is almost 30 years old and is the Netherland's biggest beer festival. Once you've paid your €5, there are over 50 bocks to try. Have fun, but be careful or you might find yourself praying to the porcelain goddess. (Map Area D4)

De Bierkoning (The Beer King) - Paleisstraat 125, ☎ 625-2336

www.bierkoning.nl

It's not a bar, but if you're into beer you'll love this shop located next to Dam Square. Wall to wall, ceiling to floor, beer awaits you in bottles of every shape and size. They have over 950 beers available! It's all neatly arranged by country, with an entire wall devoted to Belgian brews. You can grab a cold one to go, or if you're flying home from Amsterdam, some of the more exotic beers make great presents. Check out the special offers – free beer mugs with certain purchases, and 10 free beer coasters with every purchase (hey, free is free). The only beer I didn't see here was Duff. Open: Mon 13-19; Tues-Fri 11-19 (Thurs 'til 21); Sat 11-18; Sun 13-17. (Map area D5)

Café Westerdok - Westerdoksdijk 715 A, ☎ 428-9670

www.westerdok.eu

Formerly a rough and tumble harbor front sailors bar, Café Westerdok is now a friendly neighborhood watering hole specializing in beer. Besides the 70 different brew choices they have all the usual spirits. Downstairs is a smoking and games lounge with a billiards table and a dart board. Regular Jazz, Blues and Folk sessions also occur as do gigs by local musicians and international guests. At sunset this is a fantastic spot to catch the colors changing and cop a buzz watching the huge river barges chugging down the Ij waterway. Open: Tues-Thurs 16-00; Fri-Sat 16-1; Sun 16-00. (Map area D1)

Film

Amsterdam is a great city to see a movie. Films are shown in their native tongues, never dubbed --the Dutch use subtitles. That's one reason people speak English so well here, as opposed to say.. Italy, where dubbing is incessant.

Prices at the mainstream theaters range from €8 to €12 with evenings, weekends, and holidays the most expensive. Students with an ISIC card get a discount. And the City, Munt, and Tuschinski sometimes offer cheaper morning screenings.

Like cities worldwide, big chains are driving most independent Amsterdam theaters out of business, but the few still managing to hang on are included below.

For movie listings pick up the Film Agenda, a free weekly listing of what's playing. It's published every Thursday and is available in bars and theaters. Each of the big commercial cinemas also posts a schedule of all current first-run screenings--The AUB (see Music chapter) has the schedules of most of the independents. On-line, go to: *http://amsterdam.filmladder.nl*

cinemas

Tuschinski - Reguliersbreestraat 26, ☎ 626-2633
www.tuschinski.nl

This incredible Art Deco theater opened in 1921 and has been restored to its original splendor. Prices are a bit higher than some of the other cinemas in town, but it's worth it to watch a film from the comfort of the main hall's plush seats. (Theater #1). Occasionally classic silent films are screened with live organ music: quite an impressive spectacle. Go early so you'll have time to take in all the details of the ornate lobby and café – not to mention the elaborate restrooms! (Map area D6)

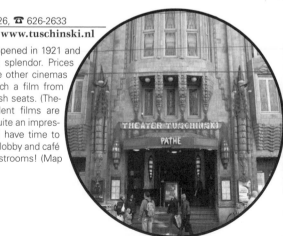

Nederlands Film Museum - Vondelpark 3, ☎ 589-1400

www.filmmuseum.nl

This museum/cinema/café was situated in a lovely old mansion in Vondelpark but has now been moved to a cold, modern north Amsterdam building. The new space is significantly bigger and right on the water, but lacks heavily in the charm department. They screen a couple of different films every day and have changing exhibitions. Pick up a monthly listings magazine in the lobby—it's in Dutch, but check where the film was made: They regularly show films from the US (VS) and Britain (GB). They feature everything from old black-and-white classics to rock & roll films to women-in-prison flicks. I had a beautifully creepy experience here seeing the director's cut of *The Shining* on the big screen. (Map area A8)

Filmhuis Cavia - Van Hallstraat 52 1, ☎ 681-1419

www.filmhuiscavia.nl

This little 40-seat cinema, just west of the Centrum over a boxing club, has unique programming like the monthly Straight to Video night featuring horror, sci-fi, blaxploitation and sexploitation flicks. Recently they had a Beer and Horror night with dark beer tasting and a *Bride of Frankenstein* screening. Cavia sells cheap drinks in their café and admission is a very reasonable €4. Most films start at 20:30. Closed in summer. (Map area A2)

Kriterion - Roeterstraat 170, ☎ 623-1708

www.kriterion.nl

There's always an interesting mix of first-run and classic films being shown at this student-operated art-house cinema. "Sneak Preview" is an extremely popular night – a surprise screening of a new film every Tuesday at 22:00 (Get tickets in advance). The lobby café is busy but relaxed, and you can bring your glass of beer right into the theater. Admission: Weekdays €7; Weekends €7.50. (Map area F7)

Studio K - Timorplein 62, ☎ 692-0422

www.studio-k.nu

International mainstream and art-house films are screened here at this east side theater/café/live music venue. It's got a fresh, local, multi-cultural vibe and there's always something happening. Located around the corner from Stay Okay (see Places to Sleep). (Map area: J7)

Nederlands Film Museum

film

Cinema de Balie - Kleine Gartmanplantsoen 10, ☎ 553-5100

www.debalie.nl

The Balie is a true multimedia center: film house, gallery, theater, and WiFi connected café. The two cinemas here show non commercial films and many are in English. Numerous special events take place here, too: organizations as diverse as the Dutch Transgender Filmfestival and the Africa in the Picture Festival present rare and hard-to-find films. Talks and debates often follow the screenings. Outside is an interesting art installation: Every night from October to April films are projected onto a screen high up on the side of the building (*www.debalie.nl/straal*). Take a look as you pass by. De Balie is located just off the Leidseplein. (Map area C7)

Melkweg Cinema - Lijnbaansgracht 234 A, ☎ 531-8181

www.melkweg.nl

Upstairs at the Melkweg (see Live Venues, Music chapter), there's a small cinema that shows intriguing retrospectives – films by Cronenberg, classic porn, martial arts and music features, for instance. Films cost €6 and usually start at 20:00. Sometimes they have midnight screenings too. (Map area C7)

The Movies - Haarlemmerdijk 161, ☎ 638-6016

www.themovies.nl

A mix of new mainstream and art films play in the four halls comprising this theater. This is Amsterdam's oldest working cinema--the Art Deco lobby and bar are like a lush time capsule from a past era. Admission: €8. (Map area C2)

Cinecenter - Lijnbaansgracht 236, ☎ 623-6615

www.cinecenter.nl

On Sunday mornings at 11:00 the two small theaters here screen new features for only €5. The program consists mostly of foreign films, so make sure to confirm that the subtitles are in English. Cinecenter is located right across from the Melkweg (see above). (Map area C7)

de Uitkijk - Prinsengracht 452, ☎ 623-7460

www.uitkijk.nl

When it opened in 1929, de Uitkijk was only the fourth art-house cinema in Europe. With help from

some excellent volunteers they still show arty first-run stuff most big theaters ignore. And with the addition of digital screening capabilities they now offer even more alternative content. The Jewish Film Festival (*www.joodsfilmfestival.nl*) takes place here in November. It's located right off the Leidsestraat. (Map area C7)

Rialto - Ceintuurbaan 338, ☎ 676-8700

www.rialtofilm.nl

The Rialto is another independent partly run by volunteers. It's located just south of the Albert Cuyp market (see Shopping chapter). They show some interesting – but mostly foreign – films in their two theaters, so remember to check the language of the subtitles. Admission is €7.50 Mon-Thurs and €8.50 on the weekend. On Friday afternoons at 17:00 persons under 25 years of age can attend the Rialto's special Moviezone feature (*www.moviezone.nl*) for only €4.50. In August they sometimes show free films outdoors in the Heinekenplein.

Smart Cinema - Arie Biemondstraat 101-111, ☎ 427-5951

www.smartprojectspace.net

Located in part of a former hospital that now houses the Smart Project Space, the Smart Cinema shows experimental films and videos as well as "alternative" Hollywood films (Coen Brothers, David Lynch) in two comfortable small halls. There are free video screenings here every Wednesday and Sunday afternoon. (Map area A7)

Biotoom 301 - Overtoom 301, ☎ 778-1145

www.ot301.nl

This 100-seat cinema is just one of the many cool projects happening at the OT301 squat (see Party Venues, Music chapter). Films are shown a couple of days a week–programming runs from classics to political documentaries to experimental films. Walk to the back of the building and up the stairs where the theater and bar are ready to entertain your brains and livers. Admission is just €3, or €4 for a double feature. (Map area A7)

Tropeninstituut Theater - Linneausstraat 2, ☎ 568-8500

www.kit.nl/tropenmuseum

This theater attached to the Tropenmuseum shows rarely-screened international films often complementing special exhibits and presented in series – a month of comedies from Iran, for example. The subtitles are usually in English, but call or check their website to make sure. Admission: €6. (Map area H7)

De Munt - Vijzelstraat 16

De Munt, named after Amsterdam's historic mint right across the street, is a megaplex with 13 halls showing the standard Hollywood fare. But on Tuesdays all films are €6 instead of the regular €9. And films shown before noon are only €4.50. It's modern, clean and comfortable. (Map area D6)

The City - Leidseplein, ☎ 623-4570

This cinema is totally mainstream, but the giant screen in Theater #1 is great for big special effects movies. Go to the Jamin candy store around the corner at Leidsestraat 98 to get your munchies before the film. (Map area C7)

Imax - Arena Boulevard 600

www.patheimax.nl

Though not as big as most of its North American counterparts, Holland's first Imax is pretty damn nice. New blockbusters and Imax 3-D productions are screened here, but the tickets are more expensive than other Amsterdam theaters. If you're serious about special effects then it's worth the trek out here for a state-of-the-art experience. It's right next to the H******n Music Hall (see Music chapter) and the giant Arena stadium. From Centraal Station take the Metro 54 to Bijlmer station.

miscellaneous film stuff

Amnesty International Film Festival - ☎ 773-3624

www.amnesty.nl/filmfestiva

The Amnesty International Film Festival is an annual five-day event focusing on human-rights issues Films and videos are screened at the Balie, Filmmuseum and City theaters (see above). Check thei website for details about upcoming festivals.

Amsterdam Fantastic Film Festival - April, ☎ 679-4875

www.afff.n

AFFF began as an all-night horror- and gore-fest but has grown into a week-long event encompassing a wide range of films: sci-fi, thrillers, anime, cult films, and of course horror. They also have director retrospectives, symposia and lots of premieres, like bringing Kung Fu Hustle to Holland. Films are screened at the Melkweg and other cinemas.

Pluk de Nacht - Late Summer

www.plukdenacht.n

Pluk de Nacht (Pluck the Night) is a free, open-air mini-festival that takes place every August at the former Amsterdam Plage, an Amsterdam beach area now being converted to a grand café. Each nigh over an 11-day period, international feature films and shorts are projected onto a giant screen. Almos all of them are in English or have English subtitles. Drinks and food are available and they have othe fun stuff going on during the festival like old-school Pong tournaments. Recently this festival has also

held indoor screenings at other theaters like the Kriterion. From Centraal Station you can take bus 48 and get off at Barentzplein, or you can walk it in about 25 minutes. Check their website for the next Pluk de Nacht location…hopefully they won't lose their amazing outdoor home! (Map area D1)

International Documentary Film Festival (IDFA) - Late November, ☎ 627-3329
www.idfa.nl

If you're visiting town during blustery November, look out for info on this famous festival. It's the biggest of its kind, with over 300 documentary films screened at several theaters around Amsterdam. Special events include film-maker retrospectives and programs like "Docs Around the Clock" – a whole night of films with a morning breakfast buffet.. You can find the program at the AUB (see Music chapter) and De Balie (see above).

Shadow Documentary Film Festival - Late November
www.shadowfestival.nl

This festival runs parallel to IDFA but focuses on more experimental documentaries, often by unknown directors. Films are shown in the intimate Melkweg Cinema, as well as the Uitkijk and Filmmuseum (see above), and the public can meet and talk with the film-makers after each screening.

Black Soil International Hiphop Film Festival - Late November
www.blacksoil.com

All things hip-hop are covered in this long-weekend festival of film, music, workshops and parties. The Balie (see above) hosts this event with contributions from an international array of artists. Check their website for location information, Sometimes they throw this multimedia bash in other Dutch cities, like Rotterdam. Expect DJs, MCs. graffiti, and break dancers galore.

Africa in the Picture - Early October
www.africainthepicture.nl

This annual festival, featuring African produced full-length films, documentaries, shorts and anime, was the first in Europe. Since 1987 organizers have brought films created in Zambia, Ghana and 59 other African countries to appreciative multi-ethnic Amsterdam crowds. This year, the screenings were held at the Ketelhuis and other locations.

Roze Filmdagen (Pink Film Days) - Every other December (even years)
www.rozefilmdagen.nl

In the past, themes at this gay-and-lesbian film fest have run from horror to religion to the "inevitable fate" of homosexual characters in movies. And of course there's always some porn. Though some of the program is culled from other, bigger festivals, it remains a somewhat underground event and a good opportunity to catch rarely screened works. Films and videos are shown at the Cavia, Balie and the Filmmuseum (see above).

De Filmcorner - Marnixstraat 263, ☎ 624 1974

This little shop is packed with cheap used videos and films. They're mostly porno, but there's also weird shit like super-8 Bruce Lee films and Jerry Lewis movies dubbed into German. Open: Mon-Fri 9-12 and 13-17:30; Sat 9-16. (Map area B4)

The Silver Screen - Haarlemmerdijk 94, ☎ 638-1341
www.silverscreen.nl

DVDs, videos, laser discs, books, magazines, posters, cards—the Silver Screen stuffs all this in their shop and it's all about film. They're also known for their large horror and cult film collection. Open: Mon-Fri 13-18; Sat 11-18. (Map area C2)

Sex

Sex, sex, sex... anyway you can imagine--and then some--it's a large slice of Amsterdam's tourism pie. The Red Light District is always crowded, colorful, and deliciously sleazy. It's located just southeast of Centraal Station in the city's oldest district, de Wallen. You'll find streets and alleyways lined with sex shops, live sex theaters and rows and rows of red lights illuminating the windows of Amsterdam's famous prostitutes. This area is much safer than it used to be, but women wandering alone sometimes get hassled and may want to tour this part of town during the day. Everyone should watch out for pickpockets. Amsterdam's City Council is trying to "clean up" this centuries-old area by kicking out prostitutes and opening fashion boutiques. Businesses in the area have launched a campaign, "Hands Off de Wallen," against this insane action. Type this phrase into any search engine for the latest developments or check *www.ignatzmice.com* (see below.)

There's also a smaller Red Light area around Spuistraat and the Singel canal near Centraal Station. And another, frequented mainly by Dutch men, runs along Ruysdaelkade by Albert Cuypstraat. But while the Red Light Districts are concentrated in these areas, several of the places I recommend below are in other parts of the city.

In case you were wondering, the services of a prostitute in the Red Light District start at €50 for a blow job and/or a fuck. At that price you get about 15 to 20 minutes--the condom is included free of charge. For detailed information about the area check out *www.ignatzmice.com* where you'll find printable walking-tour maps, detailed descriptions of each alley and its specialties, and reviews of shows, sex clubs, and the girls themselves.

sex shops

Sex shops are everywhere in the Red Light District--definitely take a peek inside one. These places all carry roughly the same selection of sex toys, magazines and movies, ranging from really funny to seriously sexy to disgusting. Remember that videos and DVDs play on different systems in different parts of the world. If you buy one, make sure to ask if it will play on your machine back home. The European system (except for France) is called PAL. North America uses NTSC. Also, most of the cheap stuff is of poor quality: you get what you pay for. For better quality goods I recommend the following shops:

Female and Partners - Spuistraat 100, ☎ 620-9152
www.femaleandpartners.nl

Female and Partners is Amsterdam's coolest and classiest sex shop. It's women-run and offers an alternative to the male-dominated sex industry. Inside you'll find a wide range of vibrators, dildos and other sex articles. They're always expanding their selection of books and movies, plus they also have some incredibly sexy, exclusive clothing–the PVC and latex wear is particularly impressive. Stop in for info on fetish parties. Open: Sun-Mon 13-18; Tues-Sat 11-18 (Thurs 'til 21) (Map area C5)

Absolute Danny - Oudezijds Achterburgwal 78,
☎ 421-0915

www.absolutedanny.com

This fetish shop is also women-run, you can tell the difference soon as you enter. It's much more stylish than other nearby Red Light District sex stores. Single women and couples will feel comfortable shopping here. They stock sensual clothing for men and women, bizarre DVDs and lots of S/M accessories. The owner, Danny, designs a lot of the clothes herself. Open: Daily 11-21. (Map area E5)

Condomerie Het Gulden Vlies - Warmoesstraat 141, ☎ 627-4174
www.condomerie.com

This was the world's very first condomerie– and what a selection! There's also an amusing display of condom boxes and wrappers (see Museums chapter). The laid-back atmosphere here makes the necessary task of buying and using condoms more entertaining. Open: Mon-Sat 11-18. (Map area D4)

Nolly's Sexboetiek - Sarphatipark 99, ☎ 673-4757

In the back of Nolly's a friend of mine found a bunch of cheap, dusty, straight and gay Super-8 and 8mm films from the '60s and '70s– interesting for collectors. Nolly also has a big selection of magazines, some not available in the Red Light District. Open: Mon-Fri 10-18; Sat 10-17.

Blue and White - Ceintuurbaan 248, ☎ 610-1741

Not far from Nolly's is another sex shop in the Albert Cuyp Market neighborhood (see Markets, Shopping chapter). Blue and White has been open 30 years and has all the required stuff plus a bargain bin full of dildos, toys and discount videos. Open: Mon-Fri 9:30-18 (Thurs 'til 21); Sat 12-17.

Miranda Sex Videotheek - Ceintuurbaan 354, ☎ 470-8130

This store boasts over 10,000 videos. Its two floors are loaded with more porn than you can shake a stick at. You'll find just about every kink and perversion imaginable, and probably some that you can't. Open: Daily 10-23.

The Bronx - Kerkstraat 53, ☎ 623-1548
www.bronx.nl

The Bronx is a sex shop for gay men with an impressive collection of books, magazines and DVDs – including a section dedicated solely to queer skateboarding films. There are also leather goods, sex toys and the world's seemingly largest butt plug! In the back there are some private cabins. Bronx is open: Daily 12-24. (Map area C6)

peep shows and live sex

Several peep-show places are scattered around the Red Light District. In a room the size of a telephone booth a two-euro coin sends a window up and you see 90 seconds worth of a young couple fucking. It's not very passionate, but they're definitely, like, doing it. Sit-down video peep show booths also cost two euros. There is a built-in control panel with channel-changer and choice of over 150 videos. Everything is there, including bestiality, scat, and roman showers. There were mostly men peeping, obviously, but there were also some couples looking around. If you're curious, you should go check it out: nobody knows you here anyway.

Sex Palace - Oudezijds Achterburgwal 84 (Map area E5)

Sexyland - St. Annendwarsstraat 4 (Map area E4)

In the name of research I also saw a few sex shows. At some you can bargain with the doorman and the average admission price ends up being about €20. Inside an appropriately trashy little theater, women strip to loud disco music. Sometimes they get someone from the audience to participate by removing lingerie or inserting a vibrator. Then a couple will have sex. It's very mechanical and not very exciting. At other shows, like Casa Rosso (Oudezijds Achterburgwal 106; 627-8954; www.casarosso.com), you pay a set price of €30 (or €45 including 4 drinks) to sit in a clean, comfortable theater and watch better-looking strippers and couples. Again, it's not really sexy, but the show is more entertaining, like the couple who do a choreographed routine to Mozart's Requiem – very dramatic!

miscellaneous sex stuff

Fetish Parties

Amsterdam is famous for its fetish parties, where people can dance and socialize in an open manner as well as enjoy the dungeons, darkrooms and play areas provided. There's always a strict dress code – leather, latex, etc. For a listing in English of all the parties around town, go online to Fetish Lights (*www.fetishlights.nl*) or pick up flyers at Female and Partners (see above). Kinky Salon throws parties mixing fetish, burlesque and fancy dress. They offer party revelers who are "...vanilla or kinky, people of gender, queer, straight, bi or try-sexual" to "...engage in our artistic and erotic world." Currently they're using the Akhnaton as a venue. (see Music, p.113) (*www.kinkysalonamsterdam.nl*)

Prostitution Information Centre (PIC) - Enge Kerksteeg 3, ☎ 420-7328

www.pic amsterdam.com

The PIC offers advice and information about prostitution in the Netherlands to tourists, prostitutes, their clients or anyone else interested. It's located in the Red Light District's Wallenwinkel (*www.dewallenwinkel.nl*) and is open to the public. Inside you'll find pamphlets, flyers and books about all aspects of prostitution. They also organize renowned area tours. Open: Tues-Sat 12-19. (Map area E4)

Same Place - Nassaukade 120, ☎ 475-1981

http://www.sameplace.nl

Sex clubs abound in Amsterdam, but this one is unique billing itself as a "woman-friendly erotic dance café." Everyone is welcome: singles, couples, dykes, fags, fetishists, exhibitionists, transsexuals… but dress up. They have piercing and body-painting nights, kinky parties in their cellar (which has a dark-room and S/M corner), and sometimes women-only parties. Monday nights are men only. Sunday nights are for couples. Open: Sun-Mon 20-3; Tues-Sat 22-4. (Map area B4)

Women of the World - ☎ 584-9651

www.womenoftheworld.nl

This fully legal escort service is owned and run by women, and has an excellent reputation. WOW's belief is the escort's personality is equally important as her body during a successful sensual encounter--and it shows in their hiring policies. All the women who work for WOW are well educated, intelligent and imaginative. And hot, of course – check out the profiles on their site. If you go in for this sort of thing and have the money (it's very expensive), these are the sex workers to support: women who have taken control of their chosen profession. Couples are also welcome to call.

a note about prostitution

Because prostitution in the Netherlands has not been forced underground, it is one of the world's safest havens for sex-trade workers and their clientele. Prostitution's status changed from "decriminalized" (subject to pragmatically suspended laws, as with soft drugs) to "legalized" (subject to the same laws as any business).

In spite of this progressive legal climate, however, sex-trade workers remain socially stigmatized and are often still exploited. They're required to pay income tax yet have difficulty opening bank accounts or arranging insurance policies if they're honest about their work. As a result, many of them lead a double life, one of the reasons they have such a strong aversion to being photographed. (Don't do it: you're asking for trouble—your camera getting smashed will be the least of your worries.)

Prostitutes in the Netherlands are not required by law to undergo STD testing. This situation is strongly supported by the prostitutes' union (The Red Thread) and groups that work to ensure sex-trade workers human rights.

Dictionary

Note: "g" is pronounced like a low growl, like the noise you make when you try to scratch an itch at the back of your throat, like the ch in Chanukah. I'll use "gh" in my attempt at the phonetic spellings. Good luck (you'll need it).

hello / goodbye	= dag (dagh)
see ya	= tot ziens (tote zeens)
thank you	= dank je wel / bedankt (dahnk ye vel / bidahnkt)
you're welcome /please	= alsjeblieft (allsh yuhbleeft)
fuck off	= rot op
do you speak english?	= spreekt uw engels? (spreykt oo angles)
how much does that cost?	= hoe veel kost dat? (hoo feyl cost dat)

free	= gratis (ghrah tis)
stoned as a shrimp	= stoned als een garnaal
got a light?	= vuurtje? (foortchye)
rolling paper	= vloeitje (flu ee chye)
to smoke grass	= blow
to blowjob	= pijpen (pie pen)
to cunnilingus	= beffen
store	= winkel (veenkel)
delicious	= lekker

dictionary

food, to eat, meal = eten (ayten)

rice / noodles = nasi / bami (in Indonesian restaurants)

without meat = zonder vlees (zonder flays)

bon apetit = eet smakelijk (ate sma ke lik)

dessert = toetje (too chye)

cosy = gezellig (ghezeligh)

really? = echt waar? (eght var)

what a drag = wat jammer (vaht yahmmer)

juice = sap

cheers = proost

watch out = pas op

squat = kraak (krahk)

fag = nicht (nickte)

dykes = potten

Cinderella = Assepoester (ass-uh-poo-ster)

bicycle = fiets (feets)

canal = gracht (ghrahght)

square = plein (plane)

left = links (leenks)

right = rechts

asshole! = klootzak! (literally "scrotum" or "ball bag"; kloat zak)

I practice safe sex = Ik vrij veilig (Ik fry file igh)

---

1 = een (eyn)
2 = twee (tvey)
3 = drie (dree)
4 = vier (feer)
5 = vijf (fife)
6 = zes (zes)
7 = zeven (zeven)
8 = acht (ahcht)
9 = negen (nayghen)
10 = tien (teen)

Days:

mon = ma (maandag)
tues = di (dinsdag)
wed = wo(woensdag)
thurs = do (donderdag)
fri = vri (vrijdag)
sat = za (zaterdag)
sun = zo (zondag)

1 ounce = 28 grams
1 kilo =2.2 pounds

Temperatures:

F	C
104	= 40
95	= 35
86	= 30
77	= 25
68	= 20
59	= 15
50	=10
41	= 5
32	= 0
23	= 5
14	= 10
5	= 15
- 4	= 20
-13	= 25

cold = koud (cowd)
hot = heet (hate)
rain = regen (ray ghen)

Time:

12 noon	12:00
1 pm	13:00
2 pm	14:00
3 pm	15:00
4 pm	16:00
5 pm	17:00
6 pm	18:00
7 pm	19:00
8 pm	20:00
9 pm	21:00
10 pm	22:00
11 pm	23:00
12 midnight	00:00
1 am	01:00
2 am	02:00
3 am	03:00
	etc..

what time is it? = hoe laat is het (who laht is het)

Phone numbers

emergency & health

Emergency: (police, ambulance, fire) 112

Police: (non emergency) 0900-8844

First Aid: (OLVG Hospital, 1st Oosterparkstraat 179) 599-9111

Crisis Help Line: (24 hours; if you get a message, they're talking with someone else who's in crisis) 675-7575

Anti Discrimination Office: (complaints about fascism and racism; mon fri 9-17) 638-5551

Doctor Referral Service: (24 hours) 592-3434

Travellers' Vaccination Clinic: (GG & GD, Nieuwe Achtergracht 100; mon-fri 7:30-10) 555-5370

Dentist Referral Service: (24 hours) 570-9595

ACTA Dental Clinic: (cheap treatment by students; mon-fri 9-17) 518-8888

Pharmacies Info Line: (includes after hours locations; message is in Dutch) 694-8709

AIDS Info Line: (anonymous consultation about aids and safe sex; €.10/min) 0900 204-2040

STD Clinic: (free and anonymous treatment; GG&GD, Groenburgwal 44; mon-fri 9-12:30; 3:30-17:30) 555-5822

Birth Control Clinic: (Rutgershuis, Sarphatistraat 618; mon-fri 9-16) 616-6222

Abortion & Birth Control Info Line: (mon-fri 9-18:00; €.30/min) 0900-1450

Legal Aid: (mon-fri 14-17) 520-5100

DERMADONNA CUSTOM TATTOOS AMSTERDAM
Kloveniersburgwal. 34
+31020 7736614

SMARTSHOP

SEEDBANK

THE HEADSHOP®
Since 1968

KLOVENIERSBURGWAL 39

AMSTERDAM

WWW.HEADSHOP.NL

VISIT OUR NEW
WEBSHOP!

general info lines

Dutch Directory Assistance: (€1.15/call) 0900-8008

International Directory Assistance: (€.90/min) 0900-8418

Collect Calls: 0800-0410

Amsterdam Tourist Office (VVV): (€.40/min, which adds up quickly as they often leave you on hold for ages; Mon-Fri 9-17) 0900 400-4040

Public Transport Info: (info on trains, buses & trams throughout Holland; *www.gvb.nl*; €.70/min) 0900-9292

International Train Info & Reservations: (€.35/min) 0900-9296

Taxi: 677-7777

Taxi Complaints Line: (note that you must provide the licence plate number and exact time of the journey; €.13/min) 0900 202-1881

Schiphol Airport: (€.30/min) 0900-0141

Lost and Found Offices: Amsterdam Police (Stephenstraat 18, near Amstel Station; Mon-Fri 12-15:30) 559-3005; Public Transit Authority (Mon-Fri 9-16:30) 0900-8011

Lost Credit Cards: (all open 24 hours) Amex 504-8666, choose "3"; Mastercard/ Eurocard 030 283-5555, choose "1"; Visa 660-0611; Diners 654-5511

Gay and Lesbian Switchboard: (info and advice; Mon-Fri 12-22; Sat/Sun 16-20; *www.switchboard.nl)* 623-6565

Youth Advice Centre: (Tues-Fri 13-17; Thurs 13-20) 344-6300

embassies and consulates

(070 = Den Haag)

Amerika	575-5309 / 070 310-9209
Australia	070 310-8200
Austria	471-2438 / 070 324-5470
Belgium	070 312-3456
Britain	676-4343 / 070 364-5800
Canada	070 311-1600
Denmark	070 302-5959
Egypt	070 354-2000
Finland	070 346-9754
France	530-6969 / 070 312-5800
Germany	673-6245 / 070 342-0600
Greece	070 363-8700
Hungary	070 350-0404
Indonesia	070 310-8100
India	070 346-9771
Ireland	070 363-0993
Israel	070 376-0500
Italy	550-2050 / 070 346-9249
Japan	070 346-9544
Luxembourg	070 360-7516
Morocco	070 346-9617
New Zealand/Aotearoa	070 346-9324
Norway	624-2331 / 070 311-7611
Poland	070 360-2806
Portugal	070 363-0217
Russia	070 364-6473
South Africa	070 392-4501
Spain	620-3811 / 070 364-3814
Surinam	070 365-0844
Sweden	070 412-0200
Switzerland	664-4231 / 070 364-2831
Thailand	465-1532 / 070 345-2088

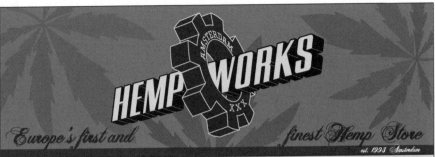

Index

ABC Treehouse 74

Amsterdam Dance Event 115

Amsterdam Literary festival 74

Amsterdam School 104

Amsterdamse Bos 14, 88, 115

Anne Frank House 12, 105

Bad Brains 109

Baker, Chet 14

Begijnhof 89

Bevrijdingsdag 96

Bimhuis 13, 111, 112

Bjork 89

boat tours 21

Botanical Gardens 11, 13, 67, 89, 104, 105

Bubbleator 69

Cannabis College 69, 71

Cave, Nick 110

Cohen, Leonard 89

Concertgebouw 91

condoms 135

Dam Square 90

5 Days Off 115

drum n bass 111, 115

Eastern Docklands 13

ecstasy 33, 84

electro 115

e-mail 64, 84, 91

Echer, M.C. 107

espresso 56

fair trade cannabis 64

fetish parties 135, 136

gaming 84, 91

garage rock 112

Gay Pride Parade 98

Goth 113

Haze 65, 67

Heineken Music Hall 110

Hendrix, Jimi 99

hip hop 113, 114, 115, 125, 133

Hollander, Xavier 14

houseboats 14, 102

Ice-o-lator 65, 69

international news 75, 90, 119

jazz 14, 111, 113, 117

Keukenhof 107

kid friendly restaurants 98

index

Kroller-Muller..107

last minute deals 7, 27, 108

Leidseplein 89

magic mushrooms...84

manga..77

Martian Mean Green 63

Mexican food..46, 47

micro-brew 123

Milky Way (Melkweg) 46, 110, 130

Mos Def...110

Museum Nacht 105

Museum Weekend 105

Museumplein...38, 90

NDSM Werf 60, 74, 93, 114

Nelson, Willie..109

New Year's Eve 97

Nieuwmarkt..72, 90

nudists 18, 95, 96,

OCCII 54, 95, 110

oldest house..89

Open Monument Day...................................104

OT301 ....42, 110, 131

Paradiso 109

Parliament/Funkadelic.................................109

parking, bikes... 13, 17

parking cars 20

piercing..80, 81, 82

Pink Point..34

Pixies 110

pool........................67, 112, 114, 121, 124

punk..85, 121

prostitution 134, 137

psychoactive plants 69, 84, 105

Queen's Day 96

Queens of the Stone Age 110

Radio Free Amsterdam.................................119

Radiohead..89

Red Light District................................ 80, 101, 134

reggae...108, 113, 125

Rembrandt..44, 106

Rijksmuseum..8, 105

Ruigoord 65, 113

Schipol Airport 8, 27, 28, 83

Seven Bridges... 111

Shark..108

Skinny Bridge...53

smallest house 103

Snoop Dogg..69

Sonic Youth 109

space cakes 62

squatting 35, 76

Street Rave 97

sushi 47, 48, 49

tattoos 80, 81, 82

taxis 21, 28, 142

techno...118

tourist office..................................7, 29, 142

trance...118

tulips 74, 107

Uitmarkt... 117

Van Gogh 65, 105, 107

vaporizers............................. 63, 66, 84, 107

vegan 51, 54, 85

Vondelpark 19, 38, 59, 88, 121, 129

Westergasfabriek.....................................112, 113

WiFi 8, 9, 11, 46, 58, 127

windmill 17, 124

WW2 Resistance Museum 106

Notes